Contents

KU-204-554

Introduction

Finland is a country not easy to categorise. Its attractions, though great, are often subtle and sometimes enigmatic; it also displays some striking paradoxes. It is a nation defined as much by its language as anything else, yet Runeberg, usually named the national poet, wrote in Swedish. The composer Sibelius, another national icon, was also a native Swedish speaker. A further paradox is that Finland has a climate that most of Europe would regard as harsh – in the north, winter lasts for nearly half the year – and yet Finns are probably the most outdoors-loving people in Europe.

Before delving deeper into the paradoxes and enigmas of Finland, it may be helpful to contemplate some solid facts. A key fact is how far north Finland lies on the world map. It stretches between approximately 60°

A typical Finnish wooden home

and 70° of North latitude, a position comparable to Alaska.

In fact, Finland can credibly claim to be the world's northernmost country. Neighbouring Norway extends further north, but a greater portion of Finland's land area lies north of the Arctic Circle.

Finland has a total area of 338,145sq km (130,559sq miles), and only a little over 5 million people. Its average of just 16 people per sq km (26 people per sq mile) makes it the most sparsely peopled country in Europe (the United Kingdom figure is 244/390). Furthermore, the population is concentrated in the south. In the north vast areas are uninhabited.

True wilderness is a rare thing in the modern world and Finland has more of it than most countries. In Lapland one can breathe what is officially recognised as the purest air in Europe.

One can certainly argue that the wilderness has shaped the Finnish soul.

TRAVELLERS

FINLAND

By
JON SPARKS

Written and updated by Jon Sparks
Original and updated photography by Jon Sparks

Published by Thomas Cook Publishing
A division of Thomas Cook Tour Operations Limited.
Company registration no. 1450464 England
The Thomas Cook Business Park, 9 Coningsby Road,
Peterborough PE3 8SB, United Kingdom
Email: sales@thomascook.com, Tel: + 44 (0) 1733 416477
www.thomascookpublishing.com

Produced by Cambridge Publishing Management Limited
Burr Elm Court, Main Street, Caldecote CB23 7NU

ISBN: 978-1-84157-894-1

First edition © 2005 Thomas Cook Publishing
This second edition © 2008
Text © Thomas Cook Publishing
Maps © Thomas Cook Publishing

Series Editor: Maisie Fitzpatrick
Production/DTP: Steven Collins

Printed and bound in Italy by Printer Trento

Cover photography: Front L-R: © Photoshot/World; © Herbert
Spichtinger/Zefa/Corbis; © Spila Riccardo/SIME-4Corners Images.
Back L-R: © Thomas Cook; © Thomas Cook.

The paper used for this book has been independently certified as having
been sourced from well-managed forests and recycled wood or fibre
according to the rules of the Forest Stewardship Council.
This book has been printed and bound in Italy by Printer Trento S.r.l.,
an FSC certified company for printing books on FSC mixed paper in
compliance with the chain of custody and on products labelling standards.

FSC
Mixed Sources
Product group from well-managed
forests and recycled wood or fibre

Cert no. CQ-COC-000012
www.fsc.org
© 1996 Forest Stewardship Council

Finns have a closer relationship with nature than most other Europeans. This is seen in the planning of towns and suburbs, in the vast number of simple country cabins owned by city dwellers, and in the general affinity Finns have for the outdoors.

It follows, then, that any visitor should spend time in the great outdoors, and Finland is well equipped to facilitate this. For those with an active bent there are endless opportunities to walk, cycle or paddle and, in winter, to travel on skis or snowshoes. If that seems too strenuous, one can take a cruise on the lakes or leave the hard work to eager husky dogs (*see pp134–5*). Whatever your mode of travel, it is important also to stop, to contemplate your surroundings and to listen to the silence.

The wide-open spaces are of course only part of the story. Even as the Finns love roughing it out in the wilderness, they like their creature comforts once they get back to civilisation. Finland is a civilised and prosperous country, with a high level of services in even remote towns and an exceptionally vibrant cultural life. While undoubtedly part of the European mainstream, Finland has its own unique cultural traditions, above all those of Karelia in the east and of the Sami in the north, and takes great pride in sharing these with visitors.

Introduction

The Lutheran Cathedral in the capital city of Helsinki after snowfall

The land

The colours of Finland's national flag are said to symbolise the blue of the country's lakes and the white snow of its winters, in recognition of the two predominant features of the natural environment. Alternating land and water is a quintessential marker of Finland – both inland, with lakes and rivers everywhere, and along the coast, where the waters are dotted with thousands of islands. The third dominant element is its forest cover: Finland is one of the most heavily forested countries in the world.

Landscape

Finland lacks spectacular mountains, but its ice-fretted landscape is often undulating and rocky. The southern half of the country is generally low-lying; the highest point is Ukko-Koli at just 347m (1,138ft) above sea level. With a relative lack of high vantage points, it is usually a view over water that revitalises the sense of space, whether it be the sea or a lake.

With a deeply indented shoreline and myriad islands, Finland has a large coastal area. Most of the coast is rocky and there are not too many sandy beaches, but the chains of islands create some of the loveliest seascapes on earth. The greatest archipelagos are those of Turku and Åland, which, between them, almost join Finland and Sweden. But groups of islands stretch along most of the Finnish coast: along the south coast, facing the Gulf of Finland, and much of the west, along the Gulf of Bothnia. Only in the northern part

of the Bothnian coastline are islands more thinly scattered.

Islands also stipple the surface of many of Finland's lakes, of which there are officially 187,888. (One can't help wondering who counted!) While there are lakes everywhere, the greatest concentration is in the southeast of the country, apart from the coastal strip. The Lake District or Lakeland – as in England, the terms are interchangeable – has literally as much water as land, and the two come together to form a landscape of extraordinary complexity. Travelling through the region by road or rail, one never knows whether one is seeing a new lake or just an extension of an earlier one. The lakes have long served as transport corridors and, before the railways came, were of primary importance for the movement of heavy goods in particular.

Towards the eastern edge of the lake region the hills become steeper as one enters Karelia. The view from Ukko-Koli

is regarded as capturing the quintessence of the Finnish landscape. Further north, the hills become higher still. Though rarely attaining heights over 700m (2,300ft), these hill tops are well above the tree line and the bare 'fells' (a term also used in northern England) give expansive views. The change becomes more acute as one travels into Lapland, where even at low altitudes many trees can no longer survive. These are regions of few people and vast empty spaces.

Only in the northwest of the country, where a finger of Finnish territory juts between Sweden and Norway, are there fells higher than 1,000m (3,280ft). The highest point in Finland, Halti, which is 1,328m (4,357ft) above sea level, is right on the Norwegian border.

Climate

Finland does not have spectacular peaks like the Alps or the Rockies. Nor does it have the diversity of the landscape of Britain. The main elements are more or less the same throughout: rocks, water and trees. Regional variations are subtle. Where Finland does have dramatic contrasts is in its seasons.

Above all it has its winters. Temperatures of –20°C (–4°F) and sometimes –30° C (–22°F) may not impress natives of Wisconsin or Alberta, but the Finnish winter lasts much longer, and in the north the sun disappears completely for a period. The British visitor may well conclude that Britain, certainly England, doesn't have real winters at all.

The winter is intense, but Finns don't hide from it. Snow covers the land for months on end: many Finnish resorts claim you can ski from October until May. Lakes are frozen and become highways for skiers and snowmobiles.

Around the equinox, the days lengthen rapidly and spring arrives with a rush, in a brief flourish of growth and renewal. The summer is intense too, with the darkness almost forgotten. It is rarely hot but is usually comfortably warm, certainly on a par with British temperatures, and with fewer wet days.

It is hardly surprising that the Finns spend a lot of time outdoors during the short summer months with their long days. What is less predictable is that they don't retreat indoors when the long winter arrives. In the cities people still cycle to work and ski at weekends. There are ski slopes even on hills that are only 50m (164ft) high and cross-country ski tracks everywhere. There is great appreciation of the dramatic transformation of the landscape, the stillness and the unearthly glow

Kuontijarvi lake

Farms and fields of southern Finland

of the Northern Lights. There is no complaining: the Finns have long experience in making themselves comfortable even in harsh conditions.

To get the true feel of Finland, one really needs to visit it at least twice in a year, once in summer and once in winter, and one needs to spend time outdoors in both seasons. Only then can one begin to grasp the breadth of life in this country.

Flora and fauna

With such large areas of wilderness and near-wilderness, it is only natural that all kinds of wildlife can be found. Wolves still prey on reindeer herds in the north, and there are other predators too, like the wolverine and lynx. The brown bear is also an inhabitant, though the average visitor is unlikely to see one in the wild. (In the winter, of course, it is hibernating.) The largest mammal you might see is the elk. In some of the lakes the rare Saimaa ringed seal survives, and elsewhere there are fish of many kinds, often hunted by ospreys. Eagles, buzzards and a variety of owls hunt across the fells and forests.

Population

Finland's population is small, and most of it is concentrated in the southern third of the country. More than a million people live in Helsinki and in the adjoining metropolitan areas of Espoo and Vantaa. The country's two other leading cities, Turku and Tampere, lie within a distance of 180km (112 miles).

The ice age

Given its northern latitude, it is no surprise that the Finnish landscape is so largely shaped by ice. Until very recently (in geological terms), much of the northern hemisphere was covered by vast ice sheets. Several cycles of advances and retreats have been identified, with the last maximum advance occurring about 18,000 years ago. At that time, Finland was entirely covered by ice, which in places was probably 3km (1³/₄ miles) thick. The retreat began about 10,000 years ago.

Ice-carved rocks

The complex history of the ice ages, and of warmer phases known as interglacials, is mostly derived from evidence such as ocean sediment cores. On land, glaciation tends to obliterate virtually any trace of earlier surfaces and the features we see belong to the most recent phase.

In regions like the Alps, the Rockies and upland Britain, smaller glaciers persisted – and in some places still remain – after the retreat of the great ice sheets, leaving their mark on the landscape in the form of deep U-shaped valleys and sharp mountain ridges. In Finland, the landscape was essentially shaped by the great continental ice sheets, which created the undulating terrain that exists today.

Glaciers are very effective at eroding underlying rocks. Fragments of rock trapped beneath the ice, under great pressure, scour away at the bedrock, sometimes leaving marks that can be seen as long parallel gouges called striations.

The ice that covered Finland was not static, but moved slowly southward. The general direction of this movement is reflected today in the orientation of the hills and lakes. This can be clearly seen on the map

The view from Ukko-Koli shows distinctive linear eskers

of Finland, especially in the region north and east of Jyväskylä.

The story of glaciation is not only about erosion but also about deposition: having been scoured away, all that rock had to end up somewhere. Much of it was ground to very fine sediment and washed away by meltwater streams, forming extensive clay plains. Larger fragments could not be moved far by running water and remained roughly where they were until the ice melted and released them.

If the margins of an ice sheet remain in the same place for a length of time there is a build-up of such material, forming ridges known as terminal moraines. Two great terminal moraines, representing pauses in the general retreat of the ice sheets, and known as the Salpausselka ridges, form the highest ground in southern Finland.

Other ridges seen in the Finnish landscape may be eskers. These are formed by streams of meltwater running under the ice gradually depositing their load of pebbles and silt.

The cyclical nature of glacial advance and retreat implies that we are currently in an interglacial period, though many experts argue that human activity now has a major impact on the global climate and may disrupt this cycle.

Global warming leads to rising sea levels, and this is now a major concern in low-lying coastal regions across the globe. However, in Finland and other regions which lay under ice sheets, their great weight caused the earth's crust to be depressed, and it is still slowly recovering, at rates ranging from maybe 25cm (10in) in a century in the south to three times that in the north.

History

c.8000 BC Retreat of ice sheets. First archaeological remains in Finland. For millennia Finland is a backwater, with little written history before the 2nd millennium AD. However, both Sweden in the west and Novgorod (precursor of Russia) in the east have territorial ambitions.

AD 1323 The Pähkinäsaari Treaty gives most of Finland to Sweden.

c.16th century The Reformation: the Lutheran Church supplants the Catholic Church.

1548 The New Testament is translated into Finnish by Mikael Agricola, Bishop of Turku: effective beginning of Finnish as a written language.

1550 Helsinki founded by King Gustav Vasa of Sweden.

1713–21 Russia occupies Helsinki – 'The Great Hate'.

1721 Treaty of Uusikaupunki (Nystad). A weakening Sweden cedes various provinces including southeastern Finland to Russia.

1742 Second Russian occupation of Helsinki.

1748 Sweden builds the Sveaborg/Suomenlinna fortress at Helsinki.

1807 Russia declares war on Sweden.

1808 Russia attacks Finland. Capitulation of Sveaborg/Suomenlinna. Finland is under Russian control.

1809 Treaty of Hamina: Sweden cedes Finland to Russia. Act of Assurance: Finns are given rights to their religion and other traditional rights. Diet of Porvoo: Oath of Allegiance to the Tsar as Grand Duke of Finland.

1812 Territories annexed in 1712 and 1743 are returned to Finland. Capital moved to Helsinki.

1815– 1870s Centrally planned development of Helsinki.

c.19th century	National Romantic Movement, flowering of Finnish culture. Tolerated by Russians as it would dilute Swedish influence.
1831	Foundation of Finnish Literature Society, growth of national identity.
1835	1st edition of the *Kalevala*.
From 1830s	Industrialisation, notably in Tampere and Helsinki.
1855	Accession of Alexander II.
1863	Alexander decrees Finnish as the official language alongside Swedish.
1862 and 1867	Crop failures – famine and mass emigration.
1868–86	Development of Bank of Finland; markka becomes independent currency.
1898 onwards	'Russification' policy to curb Finnish autonomy.
1901	Resistance to the Conscription Act leads to disbandment of the Finnish army.
1904	Russo-Japanese war. Civil unrest in Russia and Governor-General of Finland is assassinated.
1905	Peace between Japan and Russia, but Tsarist rule is weakened. General strike in Finland. November Manifesto restores many rights abrogated in 1899.
1906	Parliament (Eduskunta) established.
1907	First national election – women vote. Old senate remains the real government of Finland; powers of Eduskunta are limited, it is repeatedly dissolved in the next few years.
Up to 1917	Finland provides a refuge for Russian Bolsheviks.
1914	Germany declares war on Russia.
1917	March Revolution in Russia. Provisional Government under Kerensky restores Finland's constitutional rights. Eduskunta installs government led by Oskar Tokoi – the world's first democratically elected socialist leader. Economic difficulties and unrest. Polarisation of populace into Red Guards (aligned

with Bolsheviks) and Civil Guards (pro-German).

18 July Enabling Act declares Finland's independence in all internal matters – rejected by Kerensky, who dissolves Eduskunta, and calls new elections. Many reject the new government. Unrest spearheaded by the Red Guards. Eduskunta votes for new government led by nationalist P E Svinhufvud. October Revolution removes Kerensky, brings Bolsheviks to power.

6 Dec Formal declaration of independence.

31 Dec Lenin recognises new Finnish government.

1918, 24 Jan Withdrawal of Russian troops demanded. General Mannerheim is military commander in Vaasa. Civil Guards empowered to maintain law and order.

27/28 Jan Civil war. Red Guards proclaim people's government in Helsinki, and control southern cities. With German aid, ('White') Civil Guards gain supremacy; Helsinki falls on 13th April.

16 May End of civil war. Short-lived but traumatic period of reprisals. Mannerheim invited to become regent.

1919 K J Ståhlberg elected as first President, defeating Mannerheim.

1920 Treaty of Tartu ends hostilities with Russia and restores territory promised to Finland in 1864. New constitution enshrines single chamber parliament with universal suffrage.

1939 World War II: Soviet Union attacks Finland. The Winter War: Finns broadly united (including Communist Party) in opposing Stalin. Moral support but little material help from other powers. Finnish resistance labelled 'Miracle of the Winter War'.

1940 Peace of Moscow. Large areas (over ten per cent of Finland) ceded to Russia in Karelian isthmus and further north around Salla. More than 400,000 refugees.

1941 Finland allies with Germany.

1941–4	The Continuation War. German forces attack Soviet Union in Lapland. Further south, Finns initially retake most of territory ceded in 1940, but a stalemate then develops. Many refugees return to their homes.
1944	Mannerheim elected President. Breaks diplomatic relations with Germany, begins peace talks with Soviet Union. Mannerheim's term is brief due to failing health.
5 Sept	Armistice declared.
18 Sept	Peace talks conclude. Finnish troops withdraw to 1940 boundaries. Petsamo area in the north also ceded to Soviet Union: Finland loses Arctic Ocean coast.
1946	J K Paasikivi becomes President, aims to foster good relations with the Soviet Union.
1948	Treaty of Friendship, Co-operation and Mutual Assistance between Finland and Soviet Union.
1952	Summer Olympics in Helsinki.

1955	Finland admitted to the United Nations.
1956	Urho Kekkonen becomes President, retains office until 1981. Promotes policy of neutrality.
1958	The 'night frost crisis': Soviet interference in the composition of Finnish government. Finland obliged to tread delicately in international relations.
1975	Conference for Security and Co-operation in Europe held in Helsinki.
1991	Dissolution of Soviet Union and end of 'Cold War'. Soon followed by treaty with successor state Russia, confirming good relations.
1995	Finland joins the European Union (EU).
2000	New unified constitution curbs powers of President, increases role of parliament.
2002	Finland adopts the euro as its currency.
2005	EU enlarges to include Estonia, the other Baltic States and Poland.

Politics

Despite its short history – less than 90 years – as an independent nation, Finland today is a peaceful and stable democracy, and an established member of the European Union and many other international bodies.

Since achieving full independence in 1919, Finland has uninterruptedly enjoyed a democratic government, while most of Europe has undergone periods of either dictatorship or foreign occupation. (The other exceptions are Britain, Ireland, Sweden and Switzerland.)

Finland can also claim to be the first country in Europe to give the vote to women, which it did in 1906. (The first nation in the world to give the vote to women was New Zealand, in 1893.) In another landmark, in 1917, Oskar

The headquarters of Nokia, Finland's largest company, in Keilaniemi, Espoo

Tokoi became the world's first democratically elected socialist leader.

The post-independence constitution of Finland preserved many features of the existing political system, including a single-house parliament (the Eduskunta) of 200 members. In the lead-in to independence there was a big debate about whether Finland should be a monarchy or a republic. A plan to offer the crown to a German prince collapsed when Germany was defeated in 1918 and the new nation was constituted as a republic, with extensive powers vested in the President. These included the capacity to summon and dissolve parliament, to propose legislation and to veto bills passed by the Eduskunta.

Initially, the President was elected by an electoral college system, but, since the 1990s, election has been by direct popular vote. The normal term of a President is six years, and incumbents are now limited to two consecutive terms.

Reform of the constitution was piecemeal until the late 1990s. A new unified constitution came into force in 2000, strengthening the primacy of parliament and further curtailing the powers of the President. For instance, the Prime Minister is now appointed by parliament. Nevertheless, the President remains directly involved in the running of the country and is no mere ceremonial figurehead. In 2000 Finland elected its first woman President, Tarja Halonen, who was re-elected in January 2006.

Since independence Finland has always been acutely aware of its giant neighbour to the east. Urho Kekkonen, President from 1956 to 1981, was a consistent advocate of 'good-neighbourliness' with the Soviet Union. It was implicitly understood that the Soviet Union would not tolerate Finnish membership of NATO, for instance.

The Soviet influence on Finnish domestic politics is harder to pin down.

Finland was a relatively centralised nation even before the Soviet era: for example, its railways have always been state-owned. The general tenor of society remains broadly egalitarian. The Social Democrats, roughly comparable to the British Labour Party, have won the largest number of votes in most elections.

Its tradition of neutrality has made Finland an ideal venue for several major political conferences, notably the Conference on Security and Co-operation in Europe (CSCE), held in Helsinki in 1975. Helsinki also hosted the landmark US–Soviet summit in 1990, between Presidents Bush and Gorbachev.

The fall of the iron curtain and dissolution of the Soviet Union prompted Finland to strengthen its links with the west; it soon applied to join the European Union and was admitted on 1 January 1995. Finland is still debating the issue of NATO membership but is actively involved in the broader Partnership for Peace.

Parliament building, Helsinki

The *Kalevala*

The *Kalevala*, now enshrined as Finland's national epic, did not exist as a unified entity until 1835. It is based on a variety of traditional songs and poems collected and drawn together by Elias Lönnrot, a young doctor from Sammatti in the south of Finland. Starting in 1828, Lönnrot made many long trips to collect the source material, concentrating on the eastern region of Karelia. Frowned upon by

The tragic hero Kullervo stands in Helsinki's Winter Gardens

the Lutheran Church, pagan traditions had all but disappeared in many parts of Finland, but remained vibrant in more remote areas. Transcribing everything by hand was a long-winded process, and Lönnrot often spent days with a single individual, recording hundreds of lines of verse.

In 1831 Lönnrot became a founder member and the first secretary of the Finnish Literature Society, under whose auspices some of the poems were published. However, he had a grander ambition: to create a single epic to rival those of the ancient Greeks or the Norse sagas.

A medical posting to Kajaani took him closer to the region of Archangel Karelia, where the folk-singing tradition was particularly strong. His travels in this region gave Lönnrot vast amounts of new material and the final impetus to produce the first edition of the *Kalevala*, which was published in 1835. Lönnrot dated his foreword 28 of February, which is still marked as Kalevala Day.

The *Kalevala* soon created a stir both in Finland and beyond. However, Lönnrot was not satisfied; he continued his travels, working on what became known as the *New Kalevala*, published in 1849. While the 1835 version was based on collected material, the *New Kalevala* contains sections that appear to have been originally written by Lönnrot himself. No doubt he felt he had as good a right as anyone to embellish the epic he had put together.

The *Kalevala* begins with the creation of the world, formed from the shards of a pochard's egg, and moves on to narrate the deeds of heroes such as Väinämöinen, Ilmarinen, Lemminkäinen and Kullervo, and the queen-enchantress Louhi. One of its most mysterious elements is the Sampo, often described as a magic mill but also interpreted as a treasure chest or a world-tree.

The *Kalevala* had an almost immediate impact on the emerging sense of Finnish identity. As the language gained respectability and began to be taught in schools, the *Kalevala* became its key text. The *Kalevala* legends inspired much of Sibelius' music, from the early *Kullervo* symphony through to his last surviving work, *Tapiola*.

The *Kalevala* also had a great impact beyond Finland. For instance, it highly influenced J R R Tolkien, who wrote approvingly of its 'unhypocritical lowbrow scandalous heroes'. Tolkien learnt some Finnish in order to read the *Kalevala*, and there is a strong Finnish influence in the

A statue of Väinämöinen, the storyteller, at the Old Student House, Helsinki

language he invented for the High Elves. It is fair to suggest that *The Lord of the Rings* and *The Silmarillion* represent Tolkien's attempt to create a national mythology, a kind of English *Kalevala* – in his own words, 'something of the same sort that belonged to the English'. The *Kalevala*'s rhythmic metre also inspired Longfellow's *Hiawatha*.

Culture

Finland has a wealth of culture belying its small population. It draws influences from all directions: Swedish in the west, Lapp (Sami) in the north and Russian/Orthodox in the east (Karelia). It can be argued, however, that the influence of Karelia and the Karelian movement – showing itself in musical cadences and in the central place given to nature and the landscape – is predominant.

It is undeniable that the most famous national figure of Finland is the composer Jean Sibelius. While this has much to do with his towering genius, it also reflects the great importance of music in Finnish life. An unusually high proportion of Finns sing or play

Sculpture of a lace-maker by Kauko Räikeå in Rauma

musical instruments. Generous state support helps to identify and nurture talent. From the traditional stringed kantele of Karelia to the electric guitar, all forms of music are well represented.

However, it is in classical music that Finns have mostly made an international mark. Apart from Sibelius, other composers who may be heard on concert platforms around the world include Einojuhani Rautavaara (b. 1928), an internationally renowned opera composer, and the composer-conductor Esa-Pekka Salonen (b. 1958).

Under the baton of Osmo Vänskä, and operating from one of the finest concert halls in the world, the Lahti Sinfonia is an internationally renowned orchestra, one among a dozen professional orchestras in Finland. With the same number of semi-professional orchestras also performing regularly, it makes for a very high figure for a country of little over 5 million people.

As a highly literate nation and one of the first to make mass literacy a reality,

Finland is also rich in writers and poets. Again, one cannot overstate the importance of the *Kalevala*, which has influenced writers far beyond Finland (*see pp18–19*). However, the obscurity of the Finnish language has been a handicap to reaching a wider audience. The best-known Finnish writer of modern times is of course Tove Jansson, author of the Moomin books for young people, as well as many books for adults. Frans Emil Sillanpää, winner of the Nobel Prize for Literature in 1939, is less of a household name outside Finland.

The visual arts, on the other hand, are not handicapped by the need for translation. Painters like Akseli Gallen-Kallela played a part alongside Sibelius in the National Romantic Movement that forged a sense of national identity.

In the fields of design and architecture, again, Finns have made an impressive international mark. In 1951, designer Tapio Wirkkala won the Grand Prix at the Milan Triennale, launching Finnish design on a triumphal march across the world. Finnish design and building place strong emphasis on the use of natural materials and on placing objects within their human and environmental contexts. These ideas were promulgated by the hugely influential Alvar Aalto (*see pp22–3*), one of the giants of 20th-century architecture.

Given that many Finnish towns and cities have been almost completely rebuilt in the last half-century, it is not surprising that there is plenty of drab and undistinguished architecture around, but Finland has more than its share of striking and distinctive buildings. The visitor will encounter many of these in their travels around the country, from Finlandia Hall in Helsinki to Arktikum in Rovaniemi.

The Opera House in Helsinki, designed in 1977 by Hyvämäki-Karhunen-Parkkinen Architects

Finnish architecture & Alvar Aalto

The most visible expression of Finland's strong aesthetic tradition is in town planning and architecture. Ironically, Helsinki's great classical cityscapes are the work of a German immigrant, C L Engel, who worked at the behest of a Russian ruler, but more recently Finnish architects have made their mark not only in their own land but around the world.

The first Finnish architect to build an international reputation was Eliel Saarinen (1873–1950), whose great buildings include the railway station and the National Museum of Finland in Helsinki. In 1922 Saarinen emigrated to America, to become a city planner for Chicago, where his most famous building is the Chicago Tribune Tower.

The Finnish architect of greatest renown is Alvar Aalto (1898–1976). Aalto studied architecture at Helsinki University of Technology, graduating in 1921. He spent most of his early life in the central city of Jyväskylä, and he established his first practice there before moving to Turku and then to Helsinki. There are more Aalto buildings in Jyväskylä than anywhere else – 37 in all, including most of the university.

Aalto's early work was strongly functional, but he gradually developed a more organic philosophy of architecture, strongly influenced by the Mediterranean region, which he first visited on his honeymoon. His first wife, Aino, herself a notable artist, was also a major influence.

Aalto's later style reflects this philosophy, which connects people, buildings and the broader environment. This is in harmony with the Finnish love of nature and the outdoors, and is expressed not just in the form of the buildings but in the extensive use of natural materials. By the late 1930s this approach had matured, resulting in such buildings as the widely admired Villa Mairea in Noormarkku.

After 1940 Aalto spent long periods abroad, producing notable buildings on both sides of the Atlantic, but he always remained rooted in his native land.

Aalto was more than just an architect, often designing the furniture and fittings for his buildings, not to mention glassware and jewellery. Aalto lamps are still sold today.

His last great building, though arguably a flawed masterpiece, is Finlandia Hall in Helsinki. The plans were drawn up in 1962 and the concert hall was built between 1967–72. The Congress wing was completed in 1975, in time to play host to the Conference for Security and Co-operation in Europe. However, the larger plan, to create a magnificent plaza between Finlandia Hall and the railway station, never materialised.

Apart from Finlandia Hall, other major Aalto buildings in Helsinki are the National Pensions Institute (*Nordenskioldinkatu 12; tel: (0) 204 3411; guided tours available Mon–Fri afternoons*) and Aalto's studio in the Munkkiniemi district (*Riihitie 20; tel: (0) 948 0123; open: Tue–Sun afternoons*).

For the real devotee, the place to go is of course Jyväskylä, with its dozens of Aalto buildings and a museum dedicated to the great man (*full details in the Jyväskylä section on pp128–31*).

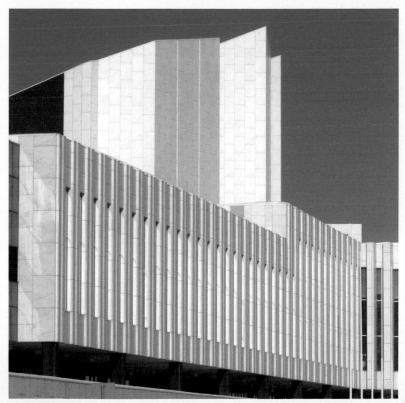

Finlandia Hall, Alvar Aalto's last major building

Festivals and events

Finland has innumerable festivals, and while some of them may be of special interest to tourists, virtually all are enthusiastically embraced by the Finns. There are far more than can be listed here; the following are a selection of the most notable.

June
Loviisa Sibelius Festival
Concentrates on chamber music, focusing strongly but not exclusively on the works of Sibelius. (Early June)
Tel: (0) 19 555 4990;
www.loviisa.fi

Naantali Music Festival
Features chamber music and orchestral concerts, mostly in the great Convent Church. (Early to mid-June)
Tel: (0) 2 434 5363;
www.naantalimusic.com

Kuopio Dance Festival
The biggest of its kind in the Nordic countries, it includes performances, dance courses and many events for young people. (Mid-June)
Tel: (0) 17 386 6200;
www.kuopiodancefestival.fi

Provinssirock
Finland's famous rock music festival, staged near Seinajoki. (Mid-June)
Tel: (0) 6 421 2700;
www.provinssirock.fi

Turku Medieval Market
Lasts a few days, shortly before Midsummer.
Old Great Sq, Turku.

Midsummer
Midsummer is celebrated across the land. There is a major event each year at Seurasaari Island in Helsinki, with crafts, folk-dancing and singing and bonfires (get there by bike or bus number 24 as the use of private cars for this event is strongly discouraged).
Tel: (0) 9 4050 9660;
www.kolumbus.fi/seurasaarisaatio/
enkku-paasivu.htm

July
Pori Jazz Festival
Another of Finland's top music festivals. Performances by many international stars of jazz and related genres, mostly on the island of

Kirjurinluoto and the river frontage, on Jazz Street. (Mid-July)
Tel: (0) 2 626 2200; www.porijazz.fi

Savonlinna Opera Festival
Long-established and one of the greatest Finnish festivals, almost taking over the town for nearly a month (early July onwards), and featuring national and international performers in the magnificent setting of Olavinlinna Castle.
Tel: (0) 15 476 750; www.operafestival.fi

Kotka Maritime Festival
Brings a wide range of ships and seafarers to the port. There are concerts, a sea shanty festival and many other events. (Late July)
Tel: (0) 5 234 4597;
www.meripaivat.com

August
Helsinki Festival
There are 100 events representing art, music and dance. It ends with a free concert in Senate Square. (Mid-August–early September)
www.helsinkifestival.fi

Turku Music Festival
Performed at venues from the cathedral to a fully-rigged schooner for an equally diverse range of music: orchestral, opera, early music and jazz being only a selection of the genres. (Mid-August)
Tel: (0) 2 251 1162;
www.turkumusicfestival.fi

September
Lahti's Sibelius Festival
Staged at the magnificent Sibelius Hall, it concentrates on the music of Sibelius, plus those who influenced or were influenced by him. (Early September)
Tel: (0) 3 814 4460;
www.lahti.fi/symphony

October
Helsinki herring market
Colourful traditional boats from all along the Finnish coast gather at the South Harbour/Market Square to sell herring and other fish. Also features traditional music. (Early October)

December
Christmas market
Runs for most of December.
Esplanade Park, Helsinki.

Folk-dancers at Midsummer festivities

Impressions

Finland is generally an easy country to visit: safe, clean and well ordered. There are no real booby-traps; you would not be committing an unforgivable faux pas by acting the way you would at home. Still, there are a few things that are useful to know, right at the start, to smooth your path.

When to go

One thing that can come as a surprise to many visitors is the very distinct nature of the seasons in Finland. This is not just a matter of knowing what clothing to pack; if you go at the wrong time you will find that many of the sights and attractions are closed.

When to visit is therefore a prime consideration, but the answer depends on what it is you want to do.

One of the many historic churches

The summer season is both fairly short and sharply defined, starting at midsummer in late June and ending no later than the end of August. The days are long, with hours of darkness being short in the south and nonexistent in the north. Many of the tourist attractions are open only during this period. If you want to take a cruise on the coastal waters or on one of Finland's many lakes, you will find things winding down even in the second half of August.

There are two drawbacks to visiting Finland in the summer, however. One is that nearly all the Finns take their holidays in this short period and many of the attractions get very busy. It is also a time when midges and mosquitoes are active.

If you are a lover of the outdoors, and especially if you want to get some good hiking done, autumn is a good time to go to Finland. In the north, where many of the best hiking trails are to be found, 'autumn' essentially means the month of September. This is when the vivid *ruska* (autumn) colours blaze for a few weeks and landscapes are at their most attractive. And there are no midges. Some alert entrepreneur will soon realise there is a great market for 'Falling Leaves' cruises on the lakes, but it doesn't seem to have happened yet.

Despite what many may think, winter is a great time to visit Finland. Midwinter is an uncompromising time, with the sun barely seen in the south and not at all in the Arctic regions, but with snow all around, the blue twilight seems far lighter than you might expect, and sometimes there is also the illumination of the Northern Lights. In February and March, there's plenty of daylight but winter still has a firm grip. In Lapland you can still be skiing in May. There are many ways to enjoy the magical winter landscape: on skis, dog-sleds or by snowmobile. You can fish through a hole in the ice and hardy souls may take a tent-sauna, refreshing themselves with a roll in the snow.

Where to go

Where to go again depends on personal interest, and all one can do is suggest a few possible itineraries on different themes. Finland is a big country and it is a mistake to try and cram it all in to a couple of weeks.

History

Finland's recent history centres on Helsinki, but the original capital, Turku, is not to be missed. One of Finland's historic towns must be

Ride through Finland's magical winter landscape on a dogsled

Sauna

If you want to start an argument between a Finn and a Swede, all you need to do is ask who invented the sauna. Both countries lay claim to being the home of sauna, and there is little hard evidence to settle the issue one way or the other.

Although the word is spelled the same way in both languages, it is pronounced differently. Most English speakers pronounce it the Swedish way, with the first syllable sounding like 'saw'. For the Finnish way, think instead of 'sow' (as in female pig, rather than sowing seed). To be accurate, you need to add a slight 'oo' after it.

However you pronounce it and wherever you place its origin, the sauna is an essential element of Finnish life. Most homes have one, or at least access to one. The Finnish summer cottage may not have a shower, or even running water, but there will be a sauna. It is an essential part of relaxing, often aided by a crate of beer.

The essence of the sauna is heat, but, unlike a Turkish bath, the heat is dry heat. In the traditional 'smoke sauna', the fire – a small furnace – is lit well in advance, to heat up the stones around it and heaped above.

When these are hot enough, the fire is put out and the door is opened for a while to let the smoke out (or at least most of it). The stones retain the heat and release it slowly. There are large smoke saunas that seat around a hundred people and in these the fire needs to be lit many hours in advance, possibly the day before; it requires some forward planning! Modern and smaller saunas are usually electrically heated but the principle is the same, though the lead time is only an hour or less.

Among the fine arts of sauna management is the ladling of water onto the stones, which releases the heat more quickly and also makes it feel hotter by raising the humidity. Doing this too frequently is tantamount to an admission that the stones were not hot enough to start with. It is also vital to turn off an electric sauna before throwing water on it! Aromatic oils may be added to the water.

One element of the sauna culture that causes some misunderstanding among the uninitiated is the 'beating with birch twigs'. This becomes a lot less masochistic in intent when one realises that soft leafy twigs are used rather than hard woody ones. It is just another way of stimulating circulation.

Tradition also dictates that the sauna is taken in the nude, even in mixed company. Public and hotel saunas may be gender-segregated, and also allow or require towels for modesty.

The ultimate sauna experience is enjoyed in winter; and when it gets too hot everyone cools off with a quick dip in the lake or a roll in the snow. Given the choice, be advised that rolling in the snow is in fact a lot less extreme than immersing oneself in icy water.

Relaxing in the sauna

included: Porvoo is conveniently close to Helsinki, but, if there's time, Rauma on the Bothnian coast is the outstanding wooden town. Tampere's industrial heritage is central to the development of modern Finland. You should also visit either Hämeenlinna or Savonlinna, if not both of these great castles. For a background to the traumatic conflicts of the 20th century, go and see the war headquarters in Mikkeli.

Culture
Again, Helsinki and Turku are central. Visit Sibelius' home at Ainola, not far from Helsinki. To understand the roots of Finnish identity, a visit to Karelia is vital, including Carelicum in Joensuu

and, ideally, Parppeinvaara, a Karelian village. The distinct culture of the Sami people should also be encountered, by including a visit to Siida in Inari. For the seminal architecture of Aalto, Jyväskylä should be included, though, if time is short, there are good examples in Helsinki as well.

Scenery
In summer, a lake cruise is essential, and many Finnish towns offer them. Lappeenranta and Savonlinna are obvious choices. It would hardly do to miss the scenic site of Koli National Park. For contrast, head north, the further the better, to the bare fells around Saariselka or Inari. There is lovely island scenery almost everywhere

Hiking in the wilderness is a popular activity

off the south coast, but the great archipelagos of Turku and Åland are supreme.

Active in the outdoors

There are opportunities for outdoor activities almost everywhere, but the most extensive areas of wilderness generally lie in the north, like the Saariselka Wilderness and Oulanka National Park. These offer great opportunities for hiking, from a few hours to week-long expeditions, as well as other activities like rafting and canoeing. In winter, ski resorts are natural centres for downhill skiing, cross-country skiing and all manner of other activities; centres like Saariselka, Yllas and Ruka stand out.

How to get around

Public transport is comprehensive and reasonably priced, and information about routes, times, fares, etc., is readily available in English.

Cycling is an excellent way to negotiate the larger cities, while most places are compact enough to make walking practical. Driving your own car is time-consuming and expensive. Distances are vast and the roads sometimes monotonous. The better option is to hire a car for just part of your visit.

Finland's trains are spacious, comfortable and punctual, but in most cases not particularly fast, though they probably provide the quickest mode of travel from central Helsinki to the centre of Turku or Tampere. The rail network runs out north of Rovaniemi and long-distance buses cover the land instead.

Those in a hurry may choose to fly, and internal flights cover most of the country, but it is a relatively expensive way to travel. It is also worth considering the sleeper-train option as a good way to get from, for example, Helsinki to Rovaniemi.

Many of the lake cruises are not just circular outings and you can travel from A to B – Lappeenranta to Savonlinna, for example, or Hämeenlinna to Tampere – although it is a slow way to cover the distance.

Finland is a land of lakes

Northern Lights

The Northern Lights are one of the most spectacular, magical and mysterious of natural phenomena. They have been observed ever since humans first migrated to high latitudes, but only in the last century or so have they been properly understood.

Their scientific term is aurora borealis. The equivalent in the southern hemisphere is aurora australis, but far fewer people witness this because there is much less land at higher latitudes in the southern hemisphere. The auroras are seen most frequently beyond the Arctic (or Antarctic) Circle but can also be seen at lower latitudes. In northern Lapland they may be seen on more than half the days in the year, while in Helsinki the number is usually fewer than 20 days. On very rare occasions exceptionally strong displays have been recorded much further south: for example, in London.

Many explanations have been advanced for the Northern Lights, often invoking the gods or other supernatural forces. Finnish folklore gives the lights the name 'revontulet' or 'fox fires'. The tale goes that the lights are caused by an Arctic fox running over snow beyond the horizon. The fox's tail drags across the snow and causes it to spray up into the sky.

The correct, though perhaps less romantic, explanation is that the

The Northern Lights are most often seen beyond the Arctic Circle

aurora is caused by charged particles, mostly electrons, streaming out from the sun – the 'solar wind'. The earth's magnetic field draws some of these particles down into the upper atmosphere where they 'excite' the gases in the atmosphere, which is what produces the glowing colours. This occurs high in the atmosphere, the average altitude being around 100km (62 miles).

The foundations for a scientific understanding of the aurora were laid by the Norwegian scientist Kristian Birkeland around the beginning of the 20th century. With a dedication bordering on the obsessive, Birkeland and his companions spent long winter months in an isolated cabin on a mountain-top in the Northern Norwegian province of Finnmark, braving frequent storms to secure the instrument readings they needed.

The commonest colour is green, but almost the entire spectrum of colours can sometimes be seen. The intensity of the display varies because of variations in the solar wind, but its visibility from the ground also depends on conditions in the lower atmosphere. For best viewing one requires a clear night without the moon, away from artificial light sources. However, a bright auroral display will be visible even against the full moon or streetlighting. Auroras occur throughout the year, but are

Green is the colour most often seen

visible mainly in winter simply because there is much more darkness then.

Auroras actually form in an oval around the magnetic pole, but because the earth's axis is tilted relative to the solar wind, the oval is not symmetrical. The best time for auroral viewing is around 10.30pm.

Many people have claimed to hear sounds associated with the aurora, but this is clearly not possible. A sound that can be heard from a distance of 100km (62 miles) would be incredibly loud, and because sound travels much more slowly than light, the sound and light would be completely unsynchronised. The explanation may simply be that the best places from where to see the aurora should also be free of noise, and that when confronted with silence our ears (or, rather, our brains) supply something to fill the absence.

Helsinki

At 60° 9' north, Helsinki is among the northernmost capitals in the world, second only to Reykjavik in Iceland. It is at the same latitude as Lerwick in the Shetland Islands, the most northerly town in the British Isles. At 60° south you would be in the Southern Ocean and on the lookout for icebergs. Yet Helsinki is a thriving, cosmopolitan city.

The best way to travel to Helsinki is by sea, threading a necklace of islands to dock in moorings close to the heart of the city. The first impression is the green dome of the cathedral rising over the horizon. One of the city's liveliest markets is just a couple of minutes' walk away from the ferry terminals, and many of its other great landmarks are only a few minutes away.

Travellers arriving by land or air will get a different perspective, but it still doesn't take long to discover two of Helsinki's most endearing qualities. It is a very compact city, with nearly all its main attractions within walking distance of each other, and these central districts are surrounded and penetrated by bays and inlets, creating space and sparkling light, and giving the air a salty freshness.

Helsinki is a vibrant, modern city, and as Greater Helsinki is home to almost a quarter of the country's population, it has all the amenities you would expect of a big city. It is also a place that has not lost touch with its past. The white Lutheran Cathedral is one of the emblems of Finland and the new high-rise buildings have not been allowed to challenge its prominence.

The city was founded in 1550 by the Swedish king Gustav Vasa as a trading post, specifically to compete with Tallinn in Estonia, just across the Gulf of Finland. The original centre was around the mouth of the Vantaa river, but subsequently moved to the Vironmiemi peninsula. The deeper waters here made it easier to capitalise on Baltic commerce.

The fortress of Suomenlinna was built in the mid-18th century to guard the harbour and the city from Russian attack, but eventually Finland was taken over by Russia and Helsinki became the capital of the Grand Duchy of Finland in 1812.

Much of the street plan of central Helsinki, and many of its major buildings and other landmarks, date from the period of Russian rule. So strong is the Russian influence in some areas, notably around Senate Square, that the city has doubled as St Petersburg in many films and TV productions. The skyline is still dominated by the two cathedrals built in this period: the great white Lutheran Cathedral, which was completed in 1852, and the nearby Uspenski Cathedral of the Eastern Orthodox Church, built in 1868.

There are many areas with distinctive Finnish architecture, much of it in a style known as *Jugendstil*. This is the German and Nordic version of art nouveau, strongly influenced by the National Romantic Movement – elegant and often whimsical. There are many striking modern buildings too, such as Alvar Aalto's Finlandia Hall (1971), the Opera House (1993) and the Museum of Contemporary Art (1998).

Helsinki city map *(for the walk route see pp38–9)*

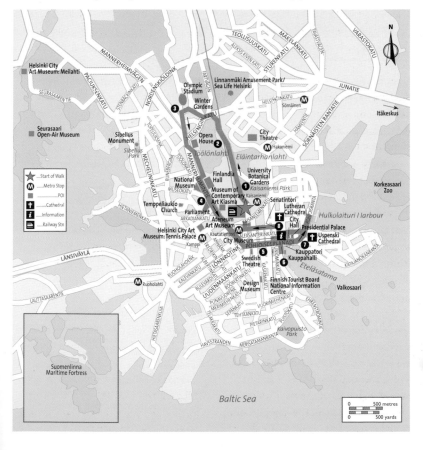

Senate Square

Landmarks and orientation

The city itself stands on a peninsula, indented by several bays, so no area in the central district is more than about 800m (875yds) from water. Important landmarks are the harbour, the Senate Square, the railway station and the inlet of Töölönlahti (Töölö Bay).

Getting around Helsinki

Most of Helsinki's main attractions lie within a small area and walking is the simplest way of exploring them. For those that lie farther out, a good alternative is cycling. Helsinki has very few steep hills and an excellent network of cycle paths. While bikes can be hired at several outlets, Helsinki's city bikes, which you can use for no charge, though basic, are more than adequate for a few kilometres. You can pick one up from any of the racks scattered around the city, leaving a €2 deposit. You can return the bike at any rack when you are done, and you will get your €2 back!

Helsinki has a very good public transport system, of which seven tram-

HELSINKI CARD

The Helsinki Card is both a convenience and a money-saver for the visitor. It allows free travel on public transport throughout Helsinki, including on the Suomenlinna ferry, and also allows free entry to a majority of the museums and to many other attractions. The price includes a guidebook (available in English) with a map.

In addition, there are discounts on many sightseeing tours. Prices start at €33 for 24 hours (€11 for children) and the card is available at many outlets, including the tourist information desk at the airport, the City Information Centre, the Hotel Booking Bureau at the railway station, R-kiosks, most hotels and large stores.

lines form the backbone. Buses cover areas not reached by tram tracks. There is also a single metro line, which links the city centre to Itäkeskus, the largest shopping centre in the Nordic region.

Local ferries are an invaluable part of the transport system. The one to Suomenlinna is on every visitor's list, as it is the only way to get to this island fortress.

Helsinki Railway Station

The Helsinki railway station is a landmark building, in pink granite. To its right (east) is located the large Rautatientori (Railway Square).

Senate Square (Senatintori)

Senate Square showcases the great architecture of the period of the Russian empire. At its centre stands a statue of Tsar Alexander II, with his back to the Lutheran Cathedral, which dominates the Square.

On the west side of the Square (to your left if you are facing the cathedral) is the main building of the University of Helsinki. Opposite the University is the Government Palace.

South Harbour (Eteläsatama)

This is only one of Helsinki's many harbours, but for visitors it is the most central. All Silja Line, Viking Line and Nordic Jet ferries arrive and depart from here, as does the local ferry to the island of Suomenlinna and the various sightseeing boats. The open-air market (Kauppatori) and the historic market hall (Kauppahalli) lie along the harbour. Just a stone's throw away are the City Hall and the Presidential Palace, a major junction for the city's trams. The main tourist information centre is also nearby.

The Uspenski Cathedral is a two-minute walk away, while, in the opposite direction, the narrow Esplanade Park runs all the way to the centre of the city.

Töölö Bay (Töölönlahti)

Töölö Bay (Töölönlahti) lies northwest of the railway station, with the rail tracks running along its east side. Though it appears to be completely enclosed, it is actually an arm of the sea. Finlandia Hall and the Finnish National Opera stand on the shores of Töölönlahti, while to the north are the Winter Gardens and the Olympic Stadium.

Eläintarhanlahti, between Töölö Bay and the sea

Walk: Helsinki city

Most of Helsinki's main attractions are concentrated in a compact area, making this walking tour quite short. It also underlines how the proximity of the sea and the inlets that lead off it create a sense of space in the heart of the city.

(The route is marked on the Helsinki city map, p35.)

Walking time 1–1½ hours.

The suggested start is on the concourse of the main railway station. Leave by a side exit next to platform 1 (to your right as you face the trains). Go left down a narrow street and forward into Kaisaniemi Park.

1 Kaisaniemi Park

There are interesting sculptures made from the stumps of trees along here, and in winter there are several open-air ice rinks. You soon come to the shores of Eläintarhanlahti, an arm of the sea. *Continue gently uphill, keeping parallel to the railway line, until you reach a bridge that leads over it. Swing left, overlooking Töölönlahti (Töölö Bay).*

2 Töölönlahti (Töölö Bay)

Töölönlahti is linked to Eläintarhanlahti by a channel under the railway. There are fine old wooden houses scattered along the slope here. *Follow the shore round to the left alongside the busy main road (Helsinginkatu) and then cross it to*

reach the Winter Gardens. Bear left through the gardens and cross a low ridge to reach the Olympic Stadium.

3 Olympic Stadium

The 72m- (236ft-) high tower opens when the stadium is not in use; it gives a great overall view of the walk route and the city as a whole. A short distance south of the stadium you will pass a statue of Paavo Nurmi (1897–1973), winner of eight Olympic gold medals.

Head back south from the stadium and re-cross Helsinginkatu. The Finnish National Opera stands at the corner by a large junction. Pass in front of the Opera House, then return to the shoreline. Continue alongside towards Finlandia Hall, then cross the main road to the National Museum. Continue down the road to reach the steps of the Parliament Building.

4 Parliament

The Parliament building is interesting inside, where guided tours provide an insight into the workings of this young but successful democracy.

Follow the road in the same direction for about 700m (770yds) to the junction with Lönnrotinkatu on the right. Opposite is Pohjoisesplanadi and the Swedish Theatre.

5 Pohjoisesplanadi

The Esplanade Park is a welcome green space. It is sometimes used for concerts and there's a popular Christmas market. *The park ends at a complex of tram-tracks, at the centre of which is the Havis Amanda Statue. Just beyond is the Kauppatori Market Square, and beyond this the harbour.*

6 Kauppatori Market Square

Kauppatori is liveliest in the summer, and in winter there are a few stalls selling hot *kahvi*. On the north side of the square is the Presidential Palace. *Turn right and walk beside the harbour for a short distance to reach the Kauppahalli Market Hall. Return to Kauppatori and continue to the right along the harbour edge. Cross a small bridge near the Suomenlinna ferry terminal and bear left along Pohjoisranta, a busy road.*

7 Uspenski Cathedral

The cathedral, with its 13 copper-clad domes, stands on a little knoll to the right. Built in the 1860s, it is the biggest Orthodox church in the west. The ornate interior decoration is impressive. *Continue to the small Halkolaituri harbour with its wooden boats; backtrack almost up to the Uspenski Cathedral before crossing to follow Aleksanterinkatu, which leads after a couple of blocks to Senate Square.*

8 Senate Square

This is dominated on its north side by the Lutheran Cathedral, while the main building of Helsinki University occupies the west side. *Leave the square by its northwest corner and walk down Yliopistonkatu. At its end you will find the Ateneum Art Museum. Cross the street to return to the railway station.*

Uspenski Cathedral overlooks the city from its elevated position

Wooden boats docked at Halkolaituri harbour

AROUND THE HARBOUR

The Eteläsatama harbour witnesses a pleasant bustle for most of the year, especially in the summer months, when the open-air market is in full swing and there is a constant coming and going of boats. Sightseeing cruises, the Suomenlinna ferry, and the large Viking and Silja Line ferries all play their part in the daily rhythm. In winter ice forms on the harbour and the sightseeing cruises are out of action, but the Suomenlinna ferry and international traffic continue. Bike lanes thread through the area and there is a network of tram-tracks close by.

Esplanade Park

Esplanade Park is a popular and lively spot. A stage at the east end is often used for open-air concerts and other events in summer. The park hosts a Christmas market every December.

Along its north side is the street of Pohjoisesplanadi (North Esplanade). Its sunny aspect means there are many open-air cafés here.

Havis Amanda (Manta)

To the west of Kauppatori is a network of tram-tracks and in the middle of these is a fine fountain. Its centrepiece is a bronze nude female known as Havis Amanda or, more familiarly, Manta. The statue was sculpted in Paris by Ville Vallgren (1855–1940) and installed in 1908. It is said to symbolise Helsinki and its renaissance in the period just before independence. Originally its nudity was frowned upon by many, but today Manta is a universally loved figure.

Helsinki City Museum

On the cobbled street of Sofiankatu, just north of the Market Square, you

will find the Helsinki City Museum. The museum has a number of specialist collections scattered throughout the city, but this is the best place to start for a general overview. There is a permanent exhibition on the history of the city. The street itself, being traffic-free, is a good throwback to life in the city in the 19th century.
Sofiankatu 4, 00170 Helsinki. Tel: (0) 9 310 1041; www.hel.fi/kaumuseo. Open: Mon–Fri 9am–5pm, Sat–Sun 11am–5pm.

Helsinki City Tourist Information Centre and Helsinki Expert Tour Shop

This is on the north side of the street, just west of Havis Amanda.
Pohjoisesplanadi 19, 00099 Helsinki. Tel: (0) 9 3101 3300; www.hel2.fi/ Tourism/EN/matkailutoimisto.asp. Open: May–end Sept Mon–Fri 9am–8pm, 9am–6pm weekends; Oct–end Apr Mon–Fri 9am–6pm, weekends 10am–4pm.

Havis Amanda fountain

Market Hall (Kauppahalli)

The charming old brick-built Kauppahalli stands just south of the Market Square, and houses scores of little cafés and foodstalls. It is a great place to buy bread and cheese or cloudberry jam for a picnic. If your taste is carnivorous, try the reindeer salami or bear pâté. Kauppahalli is said to be the model for countless markethalls around the world, notably Quincy Market in Boston, USA.

Market Square (Kauppatori)

This cobbled marketplace on the edge of the harbour was once the main fish market and is sometimes still referred to as such. It is a great place to buy fresh, locally caught fish. You may even see a few locals dangling a line from the harbour walls. But there is much more to the market these days. A range of fresh fruit and vegetables brought in by farmers is on sale, depending on the season. Tempting smells waft across the Square from fast-food stalls, and freshly brewed coffee is available too.

The Square has a good selection of art and craft stalls, with work often being sold by the craftspeople themselves or by their family members. You can find everything from drawings, prints and paintings to woven fabrics, jewellery and carvings in wood or reindeer antlers.

In winter, the market is much more subdued, but there are usually still a few open stalls and a few hardy locals drinking *kahvi* in freezing temperatures.

Presidential Palace

To the north of Kauppatori Square stands the Presidential Palace, one of C L Engel's grand neoclassical buildings. Once used as the Tsar's residence on his visits to Helsinki, after independence it became the official residence of the President of Finland. The President does not live here any more and the palace is used only for state occasions. It can be visited as part of a group tour, but only by prior arrangement.

Uspenski Cathedral

Opposite the fish market, on a granite knoll, stands this imposing red-brick cathedral with its copper-clad 'onion domes'. Its uncompromisingly Byzantine-Russian style makes it one of the most unusual buildings in Helsinki. Designed by the Russian architect Aleksei Gornostajev between 1862 and 1868, it was modelled on a 16th-century church near Moscow in Russia. It is the biggest Russian Orthodox church in western Europe.

Standing directly in front of the cathedral, it is hard to get a proper perspective of its complex roof structure. There are 13 golden onion domes in all, representing Christ and the Apostles. One of the best vantage-points from which to view the cathedral is the Suomenlinna ferry; Viking Line passengers get an even better view as they arrive at or leave the port.

If the exterior of the cathedral is exotic to western eyes, the interior is even more opulent. Four massive granite pillars support the main dome. Almost every square inch is richly decorated; the centrepiece is a great gilded altar screen. There is no seating; the congregation has to stand during the service.
Kanavakatu 1, 00160 Helsinki.
Tel: (0) 9 634 267.

AROUND SENATINTORI (SENATE SQUARE)

Senate Square measures approximately 100m by 165m (110 by 180yds). Though not particularly large, it still ranks as one of the finest and most harmonious urban spaces in Europe. It embodies the vision of the Tsar's town planner, Johan Albrecht Ehrenström, and the skills of his principal architect, Carl Ludwig Engel. Engel, trained in Berlin, had worked in Tallinn, Turku and St Petersburg before being appointed architect of the reconstruction committee for Helsinki in 1816.

Ateneum Art Museum

Just south of Rautatientori, the Ateneum Art Museum houses Finland's largest collection of art, spanning the period from the 1750s to 1960s and including most of the nation's favourite paintings. There is a café and bookshop.
Kaivokatu 2, 00100 Helsinki.
Tel: (0) 9 1733 6401; www.ateneum.fi.
Open: Tue & Fri 9am–6pm,
Wed & Thur 9am–8pm, Sat & Sun

11am–5pm. Closed Mon. Admission charge, free for under 18s.

Kaisaniemi Park

Kaisaniemi Park is a pleasant area to stroll. In winter several open-air icerinks are created and used both for general skating and ice-hockey games. The park also encompasses the **Helsinki University Botanical Gardens**, whose glasshouses and grounds are popular.

Box 7, Unioninkatu 44,
Kaisaniemenranta 2, 00014
Helsinki University.
Tel: (0) 9 1912 4453.
Gardens: open daily. Free admission.
Glasshouses: Tue–Sun.
Admission charge, free for children under 7.

Lutheran Cathedral

The great Lutheran Cathedral (Helsingin tuomiokirkko) is the main focus of Senate Square, and the most recognisable building in the city.

Looking upwards at the domes of the Lutheran Cathedral

It was originally called the Church of St Nicholas and was not reconsecrated as a cathedral until 1959. Engel began working on the design soon after his appointment, but construction did not begin until 1830 and was completed only in 1852, 12 years after his death. The small towers and two detached pavilions which flank the steps were added by Engel's successor, E B Lohrmann.

Above the porticoes are 12 statues, representing the 12 Apostles, which form the largest collection of zinc sculptures in the world: executed by two Germans, August Wredov and Herman Schievelbein, these were installed in 1849. Each is 3.2m ($10^{1}/_{2}$ft) tall and weighs about 1,000kg (157 stone). By the 1990s, they were in dire need of restoration; this was completed between 1995 and 1997, as part of a comprehensive refurbishment of the entire church.

The entrance to the cathedral is through a door on the left, as you come up the steps. There is a sharp contrast between the Orthodox cathedral and the Lutheran one. Apart from the fact that this one has a large number of seats (1,300 of them), the general impression here is of lightness and simplicity. The crypt (*entrance on the street behind the Cathedral*) has a pleasant café and hosts a variety of exhibitions.

Unioninkatu 29, 00170 Helsinki.
Tel: (0) 9 709 2455.
Open: daily. Admission free.

Old Town Hall

The southern side of the Square lacks any monumental building; the most prominent is the columned façade of the Old Town Hall. The façade was added to an existing building in 1816–18. It was first used as the residence of the Russian Governor-General, and later served as the Town Hall, City Hall and Municipal Court. It is still used by the city on ceremonial occasions. The rest of the south side consists of a row of grand houses, originally occupied by some of Helsinki's wealthiest merchants and now home to shops, galleries and restaurants. Notable among these is the aptly named **Café Engel** (*Aleksanterinkatu 26*), a Viennese-style establishment with a pleasant courtyard where films are sometimes shown.

Palace of the Council of State

On the east side of the Square is the Senate building, now officially referred to as the Palace of the Council of State, as the Senate no longer convenes there. However, it remains at the heart of government in Finland; cabinet meetings are held here and so are official meetings between the President and the Prime Minister and the cabinet. The Senate building was the first of Engel's buildings around the Square, with the main (west) wing facing the Square being completed in 1822. The south and east wings followed within a few years. A north wing was added later and replaced by a new version in 1900.

Rautatieasema (Railway Station)

Take one of the cross-streets north from Aleksinterinkatu to reach Rautatientori (Railway Square), which is dominated by the railway station (Rautatieasema). Designed by Eliel Saarinen and completed in 1914, the station is a notable example of Finnish art nouveau. The façade is pink granite and copper, and features four enormous statues by Emil Wikström. The interior is well worth a look too, even if you don't have a train to catch.

East of the station is the main expanse of Rautatientori, with bus stops flanking a central plaza. In 2006, an Ice Park was created here. It proved a huge hit and looks certain to become a regular feature. It's ideal for less experienced skaters, skates can be rented and Sunday is a special family day. *Open: Nov–Mar daily. Admission charge.*

On the north side is the art nouveau National Theatre. A lane to its left leads to the green spaces of Kaisaniemi Park.

Statue of Tsar Alexander II

In the centre of the square is a huge statue of Tsar Alexander II. One might have expected it to be one of Alexander I, who initiated the redevelopment of the city, but there are good reasons why the statue commemorates his nephew instead.

Alexander I (reigned 1801–25) was succeeded by his brother Nicholas I (1825–55), a particularly despotic and repressive ruler even by the standards of the Romanov dynasty. Nicholas' son,

Alexander II (1855–81), was a much more liberal figure and had close ties with Finland from an early age. In 1863 he allowed the Diet, Finland's legislative assembly, to meet for the first time since 1809. This and other reforms made him relatively popular with the Finns.

The reign of Alexander III (1881–94) was a good deal less happy. In 1894, the statue of Alexander II was erected, marking what had been a happier period for Finland and serving as a subtle form of protest.

Stockmann department store

Running west from Senatintori, Aleksanterinkatu is one of Helsinki's main shopping streets, and home to many cafés and restaurants. At its far end is the monolithic Stockmann department store, the largest in the Nordic countries and occupying a full city block (*entrances also on Pohjoisesplanadi*). You can get

Part of the façade of Helsinki Railway Station

most things here, and it is a useful landmark too.

Aleksanterinkatu 52 B, 00100 Helsinki. Tel: (0) 9 1211; www.stockmann.fi/ portal/english. Open: Mon–Sat.

University of Helsinki

On the west side of the Square is the main building of the university of Helsinki. Finland's first university was based in Turku, but after a catastrophic fire in 1827 it was relocated to Helsinki, as part of the redevelopment of the city, and renamed the Imperial Alexander University after the then Tsar. The building, completed in 1832, complements rather than duplicates the Senate building which stands across the Square. Aficionados of architectural detail will observe, for instance, that the University has Ionic columns while the Senate's are Corinthian.

The University's expansion has meant that it now has four campuses around the city, but the city centre is still home to the administration and to a number of faculties.

To the north, on a street off the Square, is the University Library and **National Library of Finland**, considered by experts to be the finest of Engel's many great buildings in Helsinki. Its Corinthian façade is impressive, but it is the great reading room inside that is thought to be the masterpiece, and considered by some as one of the finest classical interiors in Europe. *Tel: (0) 9 191 23196; www.lib.helsinki.fi/english/index.htm*

AROUND TÖÖLÖNLAHTI (TÖÖLÖ BAY)

It might appear to be a freshwater lake, but Töölönlahti is linked to the sea. Its shores are park-like, and it is a pleasant place to stroll or to sit and relax. Several major attractions are clustered around or close to the bay.

Finlandia Hall

Finlandia Hall is Finland's premier concert venue and one of the signature buildings of the Finnish architect Alvar Aalto, who designed not only the building but also its furnishings and fittings (*see pp22–3*). The exterior is notable for its contrasts of black granite and white marble (intended to signify the Mediterranean culture which Aalto hoped to promote in Finland), while

The Opera House

the auditorium is notable for its almost complete absence of right angles. Finlandia Hall was intended to be a part of a much grander vision: a modern Finnish square opening onto Töölönlahti and surpassing the 'Russian' Senate Square.

While the best way to appreciate Finlandia Hall is to attend a concert (and if they happen to play Sibelius' *Finlandia*, so much the better), you can also take a guided tour (*book at the InfoShop by the main entrance*). *Mannerheimintie 13e, 00100 Helsinki. Tel: (0) 9 40 241; www.finlandiatalo.fi/en. Open: July–Aug daily, Sept–June Mon–Fri.*

Linnanmäki Amusement Park

Linnanmäki Amusement Park, on the eastern side of the railway line, has been a favourite place with Finnish families for over half a century. It features both modern and traditional rides, including a much-loved wooden roller coaster.

There are two cafés, five restaurants and a Doll and Toy Museum. *Tivolikuja 1, 00510 Helsinki. Tel: (0) 9 773 991; www.linnanmaki.fi/en. Open: late Apr–mid-Sept daily, hours vary but typically afternoons and evenings only. Admission free, charges for the rides.*

Museum of Contemporary Art Kiasma

The Museum of Contemporary Art Kiasma is another striking modern building, completed in 1998. It features a curved roof of zinc with traces of titanium and copper, and aluminium walls sandpapered by hand to create a distinctive finish. The large expanses of glass use specially prepared blocks in order not to alter the colour of the daylight. The building and most of its fittings were designed by the American architect Steven Holl.

It houses a growing collection of contemporary art from Finland and its neighbouring countries. There is also an ever-changing programme of special exhibitions. Kiasma aims to be more than just a museum or art gallery, and to act as a meeting place fostering contact between art, artists and the public at large.

Café Kiasma focuses on locally sourced ingredients given an international treatment.
Mannerheiminaukio 2, 00100 Helsinki. Tel: (0) 9 1733 6501; www.kiasma.fi. Open: Tue 10am–5pm, Wed–Sun 10am–8.30pm. Closed: Mon. Admission charge, free Fri evening.

National Museum of Finland

The National Museum of Finland stands opposite Finlandia Hall. Its collections, begun over 170 years ago, present a broad picture of Finnish life from prehistory to the 21st century. There is a café on the ground floor.
Mannerheimintie 34, 00101 Helsinki. Tel: (0) 9 40 501; www.nba.fi/en/nmf. Open: Tue–Sun. Guided tours in English July–Aug daily, Sept–June by appointment.

The greenhouses in the Winter Gardens

Admission charge, free Tue after 5.30pm or with Helsinki Card.

Olympic Stadium

The Olympic Stadium is just north of Töölönlahti and its 72m- (236ft-) high tower is visible from far and wide. Finland's dream of hosting the Olympic Games was sparked by a strong showing in the 1920 Games in Antwerp (which vies with Helsinki as the smallest city ever to host the Games), and a foundation was created to promote this cause: a key element was a suitable stadium. After an architectural competition won by Yrjö Lindegen and Toivo Jäntti, construction began in 1934 and the stadium was completed in 1938; war intervened, however, and the Games did not come to Helsinki until 1952. A comprehensive renovation programme was undertaken in the early 1990s and in its modern form the stadium can seat 40,000 people. It played host to the World Athletics Championships in 2005 and also stages international football matches.

The tower is open to visitors when there are no events taking place

(*admission charge*) and provides unrivalled views over the city. There is also a café.
Olympic Stadium, 00250 Helsinki.
Tel: (0) 9 436 6010; www.stadion.fi

Sports Museum of Finland
Also located in the stadium complex is the Sports Museum of Finland. Video, multimedia and virtual-reality shows give a vivid picture of Finnish sport, past and present. This museum is a must for anyone devoted to athletics.
Guided tours in English are available.
Tel: (0) 9 434 2250;
www.urheilumuseo.org.
Open: Mon–Sat. Admission charge, free for children.

Opera House
The Opera House, home to Finland's National Opera, is a striking modern building, completed in 1993, and designed by Eero Hyvämäki, Jukka Karhunen and Risto Parkkinen. The Finnish National Opera is a highly rated company, and state support ensures that ticket prices are low – the cheapest seats are around the same price as a cinema ticket.
The Opera House also hosts regular ballet performances.

Guided tours of the building – sometimes in English – are offered on Tuesdays and Thursdays, giving an insight into the complexities of staging an opera. Or you can get a view of the building by visiting **Café Opera** (*open: Mon–Fri noon–5pm, summer*

10am–5pm; admission free). There is also a programme of exhibitions in the foyer.
Helsinginkatu 58, 00251 Helsinki.
Tel: (0) 9 4030 2211; www.operafin.fi

Parliament
A little further south is the Parliament building, a rather squat edifice lacking the elegance of the earlier Senate Palace. The entrance is to the left of the main entrance.
Mannerheimintie 30, 00102 Eduskunta.
Tel: (0) 9 4321; www.eduskunta.fi.
Guided tours (some in English) available Sept–Apr weekends, May–Aug daily.

Sea Life Helsinki
Sea Life Helsinki, adjacent to Linnanmäki Amusement Park, displays a wide range of marine life, from tropical reef environments to the cold waters of the Baltic, plus native freshwater species. The huge main ocean tank includes a transparent walk-through tunnel where you can watch sharks swim overhead. You can also join in fish-feeding in the open tanks. The centre is part of the Europe-wide Sea Life network, which raises awareness of the fragility of the marine environment and the dangers of over-fishing and pollution. There is a café and gift shop.
Tivolitie 10, 00510 Helsinki.
Tel: (0) 9 565 8200; www.sealife.fi.
Open: daily, 10am onwards (closing times vary). Admission charge.

Temppeliaukio Church
Temppeliaukio Church, often referred

to as the Rock Church, is one of Helsinki's most unusual sights. In essence it is a broad dome spanning a space quarried from the bedrock, and there is much bare rock still visible around the walls. The use of light from above, rather than from the sides, makes it unlike most churches. Opened in 1969 and designed by the brothers Timo and Tuomo Suomalainen, the church has excellent acoustics and is often used as a concert venue.
Lutherinkatu 3, 00100 Helsinki.
Tel: (0) 9 2340 5920.
Open: daily, hours vary to accommodate services and concerts. Free admission.

The Winter Gardens (Kaupungin Talvipuutarha)

The Winter Gardens (Kaupungin Talvipuutarha), next to the Olympic Stadium, are full of exotic plants, notably palms and cacti. A statue in the rose garden represents Kullervo, one of the heroes in the *Kalevala* legends (*see pp18–19*).
Hammarskjöldintie 1. Tel: (0) 9 166 5410. Open: daily. Admission free.

OUTLYING ATTRACTIONS

It is a testament to Helsinki's compact nature that none of its outlying attractions is very far from the centre. They are not very distant even on foot, but a bicycle makes the journey much easier, and buses and trams cover them all.

Design Museum

Given Finland's exceptional standing in the field of design, the Design Museum is a must for anyone with even a passing interest in this field. Housed in an impressive, somewhat Gothic, 19th-century building a few blocks south of the Esplanade, it also has a café and museum shop.

Temppeliaukio Church, often called the Rock Church

Korkeavuorenkatu 23, 00130 Helsinki.
Tel: (0) 9 622 0540. Open: Tue–Sun.
Admission charge, free for children.
Guided tours in English available by
arrangement. Tram 10 or bus 17.

Kaapelitehdas (The Cable Factory)

This huge site, totalling around
5 hectares (12^1/$_2$ acres), is Finland's
biggest cultural centre, with three
museums and eight galleries, not to
mention art schools, theatres, sports
clubs and – perhaps fortunately! –
a cafeteria.
Tallberginkatu 1C 15, 00180 Helsinki.
Tel: (0) 9 4763 8300;
www.kaapelitehdas.fi

Korkeasaari Zoo

Korkeasaari Zoo declares that you can
find 'the Whole World on One Island'.
This may be an overstatement, but the
zoo has over 200 species of animals
representing all the major global
environments, though naturally with a
strong emphasis on northern and
Arctic species such as the musk ox and
snowy owl. Between May and
September you can get there by a
pleasant waterbus ride from the
quay by the Market Square; in
winter, on weekends, there is a special
zoo bus service from Herttoniemi
metro station.
Korkeasaari, 00570 Helsinki.
Tel: (0) 9 169 5969;
www.korkeasaari.fi/index_eng.html.
Open: daily. Closed: Christmas Eve.
Admission charge.

SPARAKOFF (PUB ON A TRAM)

Is it a tram? Is it a pub? Is it a sightseeing
tour? Sparakoff is all three. The bright red
tram, dating from the 1950s but now with a
plush interior, is a unique way to see the city
while enjoying a glass of beer. Sparakoff
means 'Koff Tram' because the beer on offer is
from Koff, Finland's second-largest brewer.
Other drinks and snacks are also available.

Sparakoff follows the same route as the 3T
tram service, so you could see the same sights
by paying a lot less but without the beer. The
route is a figure-of-eight, though the northern
loop is considerably larger, passing to the
north of Linnanmäki Amusement Park and
the complex around the Olympic Stadium. It
then swings into the City Centre and to the
corner of Senate Square.

Open: summer Wed–Sat. Departures every
hour from the east side of Railway Square. Fare
includes the first drink.

Helsinki City Art Museum

Helsinki City Art Museum
(*www.taidemuseo.fi/indexen.html;*
open: Tue–Sun) has three sites –
the Tennis Palace, Meilahti and
Kluuvi Gallery.

The **Tennis Palace** is not far from
Temppeliaukio Church. *Entrance*
Salomonkatu 15. Box 5400, 00099 City
of Helsinki. Tel: (0) 9 3108 7001.
Admission charge, free for children.

Meilahti is near the bridge to
Seurasaari Island. *Bus 24; entrance*
Tamminiementie 6; Box 5400, 00099
City of Helsinki. Tel: (0) 9 3108 7031.
Admission charge, free for children.

Kluuvi Gallery is just off Senate
Square. *Unioninkatu 28 B, Helsinki 10.*
Tel: (0) 9 3108 7039.

Seurasaari Open-Air Museum

Seurasaari Open-Air Museum occupies an attractive island site easily reached from the city centre (*tram 4 and then a short walk, or bus 24*), and gives a broad picture of Finnish rural life over the past three centuries. There are over 80 separate buildings including several complete farmsteads, houses and cottages, and a 300-year-old wooden church. There are regular craft demonstrations, occasional concerts and traditional Midsummer festivities. There is a café and shop on the site.
Seurasaari, 00250 Helsinki.
Tel: (0) 9 4050 9660; www.
nba.fi/en/seurasaari_openairmuseum.
Open: mid-May mid-Sept daily, for groups by appointment at other times. Guided tours in English are available every afternoon.

Sibelius Park

It is not just music-lovers who appreciate Sibelius Park and the Sibelius Monument; the park is a fine open space, while the monument is one of the most effective memorials you will ever see. Standing on a granite outcrop with a backdrop of trees, its form suggests at one moment a set of organ pipes, the next a collection of tree trunks. In high winds it even makes its own music. Created by Eila Hiltunen and completed in 1967, ten years after the composer's death, the 8.5m (28ft) monument is made of welded steel and over 600 pipes, and weighs a solid 24.4 tonnes (24 tons). An effigy of the composer's face is mounted to one side.

The park can be reached by bus, or by a 10-minute walk from the Opera House or Olympic Stadium.
Open: daily. Free admission. Bus 24.

The Sibelius Monument at Sibelius Park

Suomenlinna Maritime Fortress

Suomenlinna Maritime Fortress is an essential part of a visit to Helsinki. Its Swedish name is Sveaborg, from which its alternative name of Viapori is derived. It is one of Finland's five UNESCO World Heritage Sites and one of the largest sea fortresses in the world. To call it a fortress does scant justice to the scale and complexity of the site. It was also a garrison and naval dockyard, and today has around 900 inhabitants. It includes seven museums and numerous cafés and restaurants.

The strategic importance of this group of half a dozen islands at the mouth of the harbour is self-evident. Construction of the fortress, then called Sveaborg, began in 1748 under Augustin Ehrensvärd, principally to guard against the growing threat of Russian annexation. However, when Sweden and Russia went to war over Finland in 1808, the fortress surrendered and, for the next century, remained in Russian hands. British and French ships bombarded it during the Crimean War in 1855. It was renamed Suomenlinna (Finland's Fortress) after the declaration of independence in 1917, and was handed over for civilian use in 1973, when extensive restoration began. One of the islands remains in use as a naval training college.

The best place to start is the Visitors' Centre, where you can pick up a leaflet and map, shop for souvenirs, and have all your questions answered.

Suomenlinna Maritime Fortress

There is no overall admission charge, just the ferry or waterbus ticket, but there are charges for individual museums.

The regular ferries, which run from early morning until after midnight, dock on the north shore, a few minutes' walk from the Visitors' Centre. The waterbus service takes you right into the channel between the two main islands, docking a stone's throw from the Visitors' Centre.
Suomenlinna, 00190 Helsinki.
Tel: (0) 9 684 1880;
www.suomenlinna.fi

Suomenlinna Museum and Multivision

A visit to the Suomenlinna Museum, adjacent to the Visitors' Centre, is the best way to understand the history of the island. The 20-minute multivision show (available in English) gives a great introduction. Exhibits in the museum fill in the rest.
Inventory Chambers, C 74 Suomenlinna, 00101 Helsinki. Tel: (0) 9 4050 9691; www.nba.fi/en/suomenlinna_museum. Open: daily. Admission charge. Guided tours in English available.

Other museums on the islands include the **Ehrensvärd Museum** in Building B 40 (rooms and memorabilia from the early Swedish period), the **Toy Museum** in Building C 66, a Russian 'gingerbread house', the **Manege Military Museum** in Building C 77, the **Coast Artillery Museum** in Building A 2 and the

Customs Museum in Building B 20.

However, the 'museum' that many visitors find most memorable is the **Vesikko Submarine**, beached on a rocky shore. Built in Turku and launched in 1933, Vesikko saw plenty of action during the Winter War and Continuation War, before being decommissioned in 1947. Those who suffer from claustrophobia might want to think twice before going aboard, as one of the overriding impressions is how cramped the vessel is; an impression strengthened when you imagine spending lengthy periods submerged, under constant threat from depth charges.

The whole of Suomenlinna is effectively an open-air museum and it is worth taking time to simply stroll about, taking in the sights: the massive fortifications, the flora and fauna that have colonised the shores, and the views out to sea.

There are a number of galleries and craft workshops. Many of the craft workers concentrate on traditional skills appropriate to the historic setting.

Given the amount of time that you can spend on Suomenlinna, it is a good thing that there are plenty of cafés and restaurants to choose from. Those that are open all year round include Café Chapman, with pleasant lunches and à la carte evening meals, and the Suomenlinna Brewery Restaurant, which brews several beers including an ale and a porter.

Boat tour: Helsinki

In the summer months (May–September), several companies run sightseeing cruises around the harbour and islands, and each offers a range of itineraries. The precise route may vary according to the state of the sea and the tide. They all depart from the vicinity of the Market Square. Special thematic cruises and dinner cruises are also offered from time to time. There is normally a commentary in several languages, including English.

The following description does not replicate any one tour but indicates the main sights that can be seen from all of them.

If time is short, the Suomenlinna ferry (*see p37*) provides a good impression of the harbour; you can also see most of these sights if you take a cruise to Porvoo (*see pp56–9*).

1 Market Square

Leaving Market Square (Kauppatori), there is a good view of the buildings around it: Kauppahalli, City Hall and the Presidential Palace. As you move further away, the domes of the two cathedrals come into view. The Silja Line terminal is to the right and the Viking Line is to the left as you pass the Valkosaari island.

2 Valkosaari

The lovely villa on Valkosaari's western shore, dating from 1900, is home to the NJK Yacht Club and houses a smart restaurant. The island is an official guest harbour for visiting yachts. The anticlockwise route now follows the shoreline, past Kaivopuisto Park and a string of small islands sheltering yacht marinas. The shoreline is dotted with some fine art nouveau houses.

3 Yacht marinas

Beyond here is a commercial port area, and the boat tour swings eastward towards the cluster of islands that make up Suomenlinna. Most tours thread their way between them for a closer look at the massive fortifications.

A view from Villinki

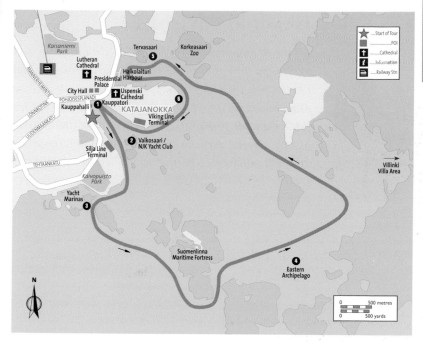

4 Eastern Archipelago

Longer cruises head to the Eastern Archipelago, taking in the Villinki area with its many attractive villas.

Shorter cruises head northward, passing a military area and a large complex of oil storage tanks, but even here there are stretches of woodland along the shoreline. The route then heads back westward towards the island of Korkeasaari and its zoo.

5 Tervasaari

Another area of commercial docks lies to the north, while to the west is the small island of Tervasaari, a popular recreation area which is linked to the mainland by an embankment lined with yacht moorings.

Heading south, you pass buildings in the *Jugendstil* (art nouveau) style along Pohjoisranta and the small harbour of Halkolaituri, which provides moorings for a number of historic wooden ships.

6 Katajanokka

You are now only a stone's throw from the Market Square, but the direct way ahead is blocked by the Katajanokka headland, its skyline dominated by the Uspenski Cathedral. A narrow canal, dug in the 1840s, separates the headland from the mainland, but it cannot really be considered an island. Having circled Katajanokka, the route brings you back to the starting point.

Helsinki environs

All the destinations in this section are within easy reach of Helsinki. Any of them can be visited in a brisk half-day, but perhaps the ideal strategy is to make a leisurely start after breakfast, to be back in good time for dinner. Each destination adds, in its own way, to the Helsinki experience, as well as to a broader and typically Finnish experience. In a nutshell, Porvoo represents history, Nuuksio represents nature and Ainola stands for Finnish culture.

PORVOO

Porvoo is less than 50km (31 miles) from Helsinki and easily visited in a day. The town is the second oldest in Finland, established in the 14th century, though it was known as a trading post even earlier. It was already a place of some antiquity when Helsinki was founded in 1550. It was (and is) a well-known stop on the King's Road from Turku to St Petersburg. Its principal attraction is the old town, with its lovely wooden houses and cathedral, but the surrounding islands and countryside have much to offer also.

There are many ways to get there. If you have a full day you can take a river cruise starting from the market place; this is a very scenic trip through a scatter of islands that stretch all the way from Helsinki to the mouth of the Porvoo River, but it allows only a couple of hours in Porvoo itself. Trips are operated by Royal Line (*Pohjoisranta 4, 00170 Helsinki;*

tel: (0) 9 612 2950/9550; www.royalline.fi/english/english.html; operates late June–mid-Aug).

You can follow the same route more slowly on the converted 1912 steamship MS *J L Runeberg* (*operates early May–mid-Sept*).

Another pleasing option is to take a Museum Train using historic diesel railcars. These leave Helsinki on Saturday mornings in July and August. You can also purchase combined tickets to travel one way by train and the other way on the *Runeberg* (*Shipowners Co J L Runeberg, Wittenberginkatu 12, FIN-06100 Porvoo; tel: (0) 19 524 3331; www.msjlruneberg.fi/index_eng.html*).

There are also regular buses to Porvoo from Helsinki.

Old Porvoo

Old Porvoo is an integrated area of around 250 houses and 300 outbuildings, presently home to about 700 people. The earliest dwellings are made of wood and many of them, like the picturesque row of houses along the shore, are stained with red ochre. The shore houses originally served as warehouses for the storage of goods – fish, wine, spices, tobacco and coffee among others – unloaded from the trading vessels of the Hanseatic League. Moving away from the shore, one finds a maze of narrow streets and cobbled alleys. To escape the to-ing and fro-ing of motor vehicles that tends to detract from the old-world atmosphere, it is rewarding to explore some of the back lanes, where, in places, the 'paving' is simply exposed pinkish bedrock. The main centres for shopping and

refreshment, and for craft workshops and galleries, are the two streets of Välikatu and Itäinen Pitkäkatu. In all, the old town area has more than 30 individual shops, galleries and privately run mini-museums.

Cathedral

The old town is dominated by the cathedral, but tragically this was severely damaged by a fire caused by an arson attack in May 2006. The outer roof completely collapsed and a timetable for restoration is unclear at the time of writing. The first church on the site was established in the late 13th or early 14th century, and it was

Helsinki environs

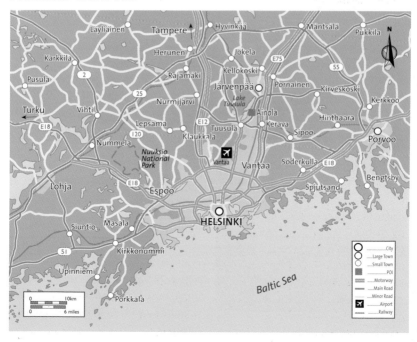

15th century to give it ~~s~~ present shape, though it ~~a~~ttacked and burned several ~~times~~ in the course of its history. It became a cathedral in 1723, and it was here that the Diet of Finland was convened in 1809, at which the Finns gained the right to follow their own faith. The simple shape of the cathedral with ornate brick decoration on the gable ends (which survived intact) is typical of this part of Finland. The bell tower is a completely separate structure.

Kirkkotori 1. Tel: (0) 1 966 111.
Open: daily except Sun mornings during service May–Oct. Free admission.

Edelfelt-Vallgren Museum

The ticket for Porvoo Museum (*see opposite*) also gives admission to the Edelfelt-Vallgren Museum, housed in a

Porvoo shore houses

merchant's dwelling of 1762. This principally commemorates the painter Albert Edelfelt and the sculptor Ville Vallgren (creator of Helsinki's Havis Amanda statue), but also features the work of several other noted Finnish artists.

Välikatu 11. Tel: (0) 19 574 7500;
www.porvoonmuseo.fi.
Open: Apr–Sept. Admission charge.

Orthodox church

Porvoo also has a small but attractive Orthodox church. You can find this by crossing the bridge directly below the cathedral and heading up the road opposite for a few minutes.

Tattarmalmi. Tel: (0) 19 584 754,
524 9854. Open: June–mid-Aug.
Free admission.

Outboard Museum

There are several other museums in Porvoo that have a quirky, small-scale appeal. The Outboard Museum, in one of the shore houses, a re-creation of an outboard motor repair shop of the 1950s, is one of these.

Jokikatu 14. Tel: (0) 19 811 134.
Open: June–mid-Aug Sat–Sun.
Free admission.

Porvoo Museum

Porvoo Museum is in the Old Town Hall, which dates from 1764. It has expositions of the history and culture of the region, with multimedia displays alongside a wide-ranging collection of furniture and artefacts.

Tel: (0) 19 574 7500;
www.porvoonmuseo.fi.
Open: Apr–Sept. Admission charge.

Porvoo Toy Museum

At the same address you will find the
Porvoo Toy Museum, the personal
creation of Mrs Evi Söderlund, who still
presides over the collection and delights
in sharing her enthusiasm with visitors
– especially younger ones. The
collection, put together over nearly 40
years, includes approximately 1,000
dolls and hundreds of other toys,
dating from 1800 to 1990.
Jokikatu 14 (inner court). Tel: (0) 50 910
2030; www.lelumuseo.com.
Open: daily Aug–May, June–July
Sat–Thur. Admission charge.

J L Runeberg's home

A short way east of the old town is the
home of Johan Ludvig Runeberg,
Finland's national poet. Runeberg
lived in this house with his family from
1852 to 1880. Since 1882, the home has
been a museum with a well-preserved
atmosphere of the mid-19th century.
Aleksanterinkatu 3. Tel: (0) 19 581 330;
www.runeberg.net. Open: daily except
winter Wed–Sun. Admission charge
(includes entry for Walter Runeberg
sculpture collection next door).

Railway station

Porvoo also has a preserved railway
running for 12km (7 miles) through
attractive countryside to Hinthaara
village. Steam trains run on a few
Saturdays in July and August behind a
finely restored Tk3 locomotive no. 1168,
now rechristened Lili. Over 150 of these
locomotives operated on the Finnish rail
network from 1928 onwards. The last
one was withdrawn from service in
1975. The station survives near the
bridge, and excursion trains arrive at a
platform opposite the shore houses.
Höyryraide Ay/Steamrail, Tapani
Laaksomies, Sumiaistentie 16, 44200
Suolahti. Tel: (0) 400 845 466;
www.steamrail.fi

NUUKSIO NATIONAL PARK

Nuuksio is the national park closest to
Helsinki and presents an ideal
opportunity, even for those on a short
break, to experience a typical, largely
unspoilt Finnish landscape. It is a
popular, often crowded spot, but by
walking a few kilometres you will be
able to find a quiet clearing and to
immerse yourself in silence. Travelling
to Nuuksio in the autumn, you will
often find passengers on the train and
bus carrying buckets or baskets, as
collecting berries and fungi is a
common pastime, hallowed by the
tradition of 'every man's right'.

The landscape was scarred by the last
ice age and now appears as a complex
pattern of hummocks and hollows, most
of them occupied by clear tarns or pools.
The highest hills stand about 110m
(360ft) above sea level, and where the
summits are bare they offer great
panoramic views. However, the landscape
is predominantly covered with forests.

Finnish forests are quite open and travelling through them is usually easy, except where the ground is swampy. Much of the ground cover is lichen. Birds that nest here include the woodlark and nightjar, along with the magnificent capercaillie, a huge relative of the grouse. Black-throated and red-throated divers visit the lakes and ospreys hunt for fish, while woodpeckers inhabit the forest.

Perhaps the most remarkable denizen of the area is the flying squirrel, believed to occur here in greater numbers than anywhere else in Finland. This small squirrel has broad flaps of skin between its front and hind legs, and, though it doesn't actually fly like birds do, it can glide for long distances (up to 75m/82yds). As it is a nocturnal creature, the best chance of seeing one for the day visitor is by visiting the exhibition in Haukkalampi nature cabin.

Nuuksio is easily reached by public transport from Helsinki: take any train to Espoo (Espoon keskus), which is one of the major satellite cities forming the Greater Helsinki metropolis. From just outside the train station take a bus (Bus 85 or 85A) to Nuuksionpää. From here it is a walk of about 2km (1¹/₄ miles) down a gravel road to Haukkalampi. Those with cars can drive all the way to Haukkalampi. Take a packed lunch and something to drink, as there are no refreshment facilities in the park (apart from a drinking-water tap at Haukkalampi nature cabin). For guided trips and many other activities in the park, see www.kaikuva.fi

JÄRVENPÄÄ AND TUUSULA

For most people, the principal, if not the only, attraction in the Järvenpää area is Ainola, home of Jean Sibelius. Sibelius was, however, only the most famous, and not the first, of numerous artists who found the area around Lake Tuusula (Tuusulanjärvi) an antidote to the bustle and stress of Helsinki, less than 40km (25 miles) to the south. From the turn of the 20th century onwards it became a major artists' colony, and still retains much of its cultural importance. The homes of other artists can be

A DAY IN ESTONIA

It might seem odd to include a city in another country, but the stunning, medieval city of Tallinn in Estonia, just across the Gulf of Finland, is closer than Turku or Tampere and can be reached more quickly. The high-speed ferries of the Nordic Jet Line leave from near the market square several times daily, making the crossing in around 90 minutes. Tallink ferries operate from the West terminal. Several other companies also operate the route. As Estonia is now in the EU, formalities for British and Irish citizens are minimal. US and Australian citizens may also visit without visas.

Nordic Jet Line
Kanavaterminaali K5, PL 134
FIN-00161 Helsinki
Tel: (0) 9 681 770; www-eng.njl.fi/

Tallink
Erottajankatu 19
00130 Helsinki
Tel: (0) 9 228 311; www.tallink.fi/en/

Take a Nordic Jet Line ferry to Tallinn

visited as well. Concerts and exhibitions are a regular feature. It is also a pleasant area for walking or sailing.

Ainola

Ainola was the home of Jean Sibelius for most of his adult life. The composer purchased the land in 1903 and the building – designed by Lars Sonck – was completed the following year. The house is named after Sibelius' wife, Aino, and their remains are buried in the garden. The house is maintained by the Ainola Foundation, established by their daughters.

In the early years the surroundings of Ainola were almost pristine countryside; Sibelius' biographer, Erik Tawaststjerna, records how he loved to watch and listen to birds and follow the changes of the seasons. Resonances of all this found their way into his music, much of which was written in the study upstairs. From its windows there is a view of Tuusulanjärvi, from which Sibelius frequently drew inspiration.

The house is modest in size, especially considering that the couple raised their five daughters here, and refreshingly unpretentious. Many interior fittings, like the staircase and kitchen cabinets, were designed by Aino Sibelius herself, and she also planned and nurtured the garden. Aino lived on here for over ten years after her husband's death.

An adjacent café is open at weekends, which also sells postcards, books and Sibelius CDs.

Ainolantie, 04400 Järvenpää.
Tel: (0) 9 287 322; www.ainola.fi.
Ainola can be reached by bus from Helsinki bus station or by train to Järvenpää.
Open: early May–end Sept Tue–Sun.
Admission charge.

Walk: Nuuksio National Park

The walk described below starts from Nuuksionpää; those with their own transport can do a loop from Haukkalampi, bringing the distance down to 4km (2½ miles).

Time: 2½ hours. Distance: 8km (5 miles).

From the bus stop walk down the sideroad signposted 'to Haukkalampi'.

1 Park boundary

There are scattered houses and fields along the rough road before the park boundary. Just beyond this the road crosses the Myllypuro brook, which is actually the main stream draining much of the park. It feeds the lake Nuuksion Pitkäjärvi, which was connected to the sea until around 3000 BC.

Continue walking through the forest, till you come to a parking area and a barrier across the track. Just a short distance ahead is Haukkalampi Nature Cabin.

2 Haukkalampi Nature Cabin

This simple cabin offers a range of information. There is also a space for resting and eating packed lunches. It is open seven days a week in summer, and only during weekends at other times. In the adjacent Haukanpesä Guide Hut, a National Park ranger is normally present in summer.

Follow the blue waymarks from Haukkalampi Nature Cabin for the Haukankierros route. There are other routes, including the Punarinnankierros route (red), an easy loop of 2km (1¼ miles). Take the blue route for about 500m (550yds) to Mustalampi.

3 Mustalampi

This small shady tarn is notable for its unusual free-floating turf 'islands'. These originated when the water level was raised by a dam in the 1950s and

A brook in Nuuksio National park

areas of turf broke free and floated. There is a platform at one point on the shoreline which allows access for swimming; elsewhere the swampy margins make access difficult.
Keep bearing right at trail junctions, following the blue waymarks through the forest.

4 Haukkalampi

The narrow stretch of water on the right is actually an arm of Haukkalampi, the same lake or tarn seen near the nature cabin. The forest around here is some of the best old-growth forest in the park, dominated by tall spruce trees. Other areas have been affected by commercial forestry in recent times.

Keep right again at the next junction and the trail begins to climb gradually.

5 Elevated ridge

At the high point of the trail the forest is more open, with bare rock showing through the lichen-strewn ground. On these thin soils the most visible tree is the Scots pine. Keep to the path as the lichen cover is deceptive and trap-laden. There are glimpses of wider views south over Haukkalampi and north to the valley of the Myllypuro brook. The northward view also takes in the farmstead at Högbacka, established in the 1930s and today the park-service base.
The trail continues rightward and returns to the car park by Haukkalampi. Retrace along the road to the bus stop.

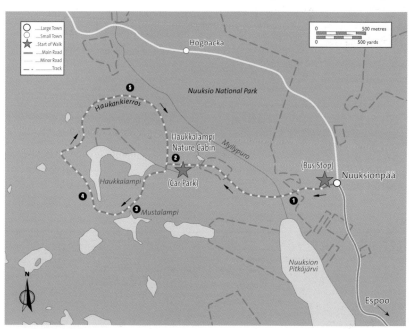

Sibelius: composer and national symbol

To most of the world, Jean Sibelius is one of the greatest composers of the 20th century. To his countrymen, he is much more – almost a personification of the struggle for national independence which came to fruition in 1917, right in the middle of the composer's most productive period.

Sibelius was born in Hameelinna, between Helsinki and Tampere, in 1865. His father was a doctor and the family spoke Swedish, as was the norm among the middle and upper classes at the time. Yet it is ironic that Sibelius, so closely associated with the Finnish identity, was never as comfortable speaking Finnish as Swedish.

Young Jean was a keen musician, composing small pieces at an early age. He became a skilled violinist, but, under family pressure, entered Helsinki University to study law. He simultaneously took violin lessons at the Helsinki Academy of Music: subsequently, he dropped his law studies and joined the Academy full-time.

In 1890, Sibelius travelled to Berlin to study music and in 1891 to Vienna, although Tchaikovsky, the Russian composer, remained his greatest outside influence. He returned to Finland when the country was in the middle of an upsurge of nationalism, and threw himself into creating compositions that would express the emerging national identity.

He was encouraged in this by his wife, Aino, whom he married in 1892, and whose family had embraced the cause of the Finnish-speaking population. Sibelius' first major work was the symphonic poem *Kullervo* (1892), followed by others inspired by the *Kalevala* (*see pp18–19*), such as *En Saga*, *Karelia Suite* and, of course, *Finlandia*. At a time when Russia had clamped down on free speech and the press, this last piece was an instant hit – although, under Russian rule, it had to be played under the more innocent title of *'Impromptu'*.

Sibelius' home Ainola, at Järvenpää

A close-up of Sibelius' effigy (part of the Sibelius memorial in Helsinki)

Sibelius' *First Symphony* appeared in 1898 and the *Second* in 1902, followed by the *Violin Concerto*. The *Third* and *Fourth Symphonies* established his reputation internationally. The magnificent *Fifth* was first performed in 1915 but was subsequently withdrawn and revised; the final version was completed in 1919. The intervening years saw the declaration of independence and the subsequent civil war which finally established the modern state of Finland.

The upheavals of this period may help to explain why Sibelius wrote few major works during the later years of his long life, though these do include the *Sixth* and *Seventh Symphonies* (he composed an *Eighth* but subsequently destroyed it). Sibelius' last surviving work is *Tapiola*, composed in 1926, although he lived on until 1957.

One does not need a deep understanding of Finland's nationalist history to appreciate Sibelius' music. While some works make explicit references to the *Kalevala* legends, the symphonies are usually seen more as abstract evocations of the Finnish landscape, although this may or may not be what Sibelius intended. He himself spoke of the *Fifth Symphony* in terms of standing in a deep valley looking up at a mountain that must be climbed, an image more suited to the Alps. But, in general, Sibelius' orchestral works are magnificently in tune with the land, from the expansiveness of its northern fells to the intimate beauty of its forests, and there is no better soundtrack for the traveller in Finland.

Southwest Finland and the west coast

The southwest can be roughly defined as the territory west of a line running north from Helsinki to about 64° latitude. This is a region rich in history, with many wooden towns, old ports and castles. There are no mountains or high hills, and fewer and smaller lakes than further east. The mix of land and water that is so typical of Finland is still evident, but in a pattern of islands dotting a glittering sea rather than of lakes and land.

The area has most of Finland's best beaches. Inland, the scenery is generally rolling rather than dramatic. The Swedish influence is particularly strong, with many municipalities being bilingual and some communities having a majority of Swedish speakers.

TURKU (SWEDISH: ÅBO)

Turku ranks fifth amongst Finland's cities in population (after Helsinki, Espoo, Tampere and Vantaa), but in many other ways, as its inhabitants will proudly relate, it stands first. It was the original capital of the country, home to its first cathedral and first university. Helsinki, by comparison, is just a youthful upstart.

Turku is a fairly compact city, but, thanks to its setting on the banks of the River Aura, it has an elegant and spacious feel.

Beyond the city itself, the scenery inland is pleasant rather than remarkable. Heading out to sea,

however, you quickly find yourself in one of Europe's most distinctive landscapes. Most of the Finnish coast is frilled with islands, but the Turku Archipelago (Finnish Turun Saaristo; Swedish Åbo Skargård) is the exemplar. The Archipelago is composed of many thousands of islands. Here land and sea are inextricably tangled and the rhythm of life is set by the time of the next ferry. A visit to the Archipelago, whether by car or, better still, by boat and bike, should definitely not be missed.

Just 17km (10½ miles) from Turku is the pretty little port of Naantali, one of the best-preserved wooden towns of Finland. It is a standard part of the archipelago tour, or you can get there easily by bus or bike.

Landmarks and orientation

Turku is an easy place to explore: most of the places of interest lie along the River Aura, on an almost straight stretch of little more than 2km (1¹/₄ miles), between the cathedral and the castle. The lower part of this reach of the river is lined with ships, many permanently moored, some forming part of the Maritime Museum and others serving as restaurants. The river is spanned by five bridges; lower down you can cross the river – for free – by the much-loved little ferry (*föri*) which shuttles all day long.

Just beyond the castle, the river opens out into a channel which, though not obvious, is an arm of the sea, sheltered by the island of Hirvensalo. Turku's busy commercial port is situated on this channel, north of the castle.

Away from the river, there are extensive green areas close at hand, while the centre of the city is a compact area between the north bank of the river and the railway station.

Southwest Finland and the west coast

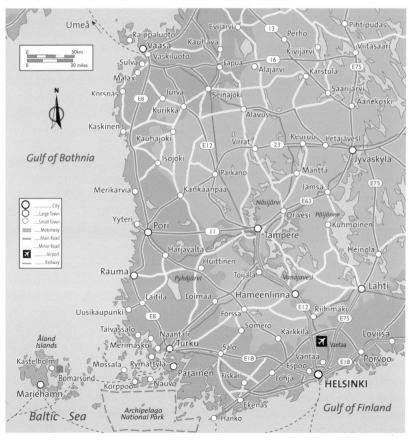

The *Suomen Joutsen* on show at the Forum Marinum

In a city of this size, while you can easily get around entirely by walking, it is useful to know that there is a comprehensive local bus network. Fares are modest, and you can travel free if you purchase a Turku Card, which also allows free admission to all the city's museums, and carries discounts at many hotels and restaurants. A 24-hour card costs €21, a family card €40.

Turku was founded in AD 1229, more than 300 years before Helsinki, and through the centuries of Swedish rule it was Finland's first city. Substantial remains of its medieval past can be seen, most notably in the castle and the cathedral. Much of the old town, however, was destroyed in a calamitous fire in 1827. The Tsar's architect, C L Engel, was brought in to lay out the new town plan (the basis of the present street map) and he designed several notable buildings.

Biological Museum

Housed in an early 20th-century *Jugendstil* (art nouveau) building that is worth seeing in its own right, the Biological Museum is one of the best places in Finland to get an overview of the wildlife of the country. Large diorama displays set the specimens in the context of their environment. About 30 mammalian species and 136 bird species can be seen. The museum also hosts changing exhibitions and other events.

Neitsytpolku 1, 20100 Turku.
Tel: (0) 2 262 0340;
www.turku.fi. Open: summer daily,
winter Tue–Sun shorter hours.
Admission charge.
Buses 3, 30 from Market Sq.

Cathedral

Turku Cathedral is the mother church of the Finnish Lutheran Church, and is considered a national shrine. The first stone church on the site, replacing an earlier wooden one, was completed before 1300, and in that year it was consecrated as a cathedral dedicated to the Virgin Mary and St Henry (the English-born first bishop of Finland).

Only a small section of the original masonry can be seen today. Most of the present interior was built in stages during the 13th, 14th and 15th centuries, though heavily restored in the 1830s after the fire of 1827. The main external walls date from the late 15th and early 16th centuries. The tower, 101m (331ft) high, was also built after the great fire. A major restoration programme was completed in 1979.

The interior of the cathedral owes much to the restoration of the 1830s. The pulpit and the reredos behind the high altar were both designed by C L Engel. The altarpiece was painted by Frederik Westin in 1836.

The chancel walls and ceiling bear frescos by the artist R W Ekman. Along with familiar incidents from the life of Christ, they also depict two key moments in the history of Finnish Christianity: Bishop (later St) Henry baptising the first Finnish converts, and the presentation of the first Finnish New Testament to King Gustavus Vasa.

There is a museum in the south gallery (*tel: (0) 2 261 7100; open: daily except during services and church events; admission charge*).

There is a also a café, Domcafé (*open: summer daily*). *Tuomiokirkkotori 20, 20500 Turku. Tel: (0) 2 261 7100; www.turunsrk.fi/portal/turun_ tuomiokirkko/english. Cathedral open: daily 9am–7pm, summer 9am–8pm, except during services and church events. Free admission.*

A peaceful summer evening by the River Aura

Forum Marinum

Forum Marinum is Turku's maritime museum. Its main buildings were originally a warehouse and grain depot. Its permanent exhibition, titled 'From Hoy to Ro-Ro, from Galley to Hovercraft' (it sounds pithier in Finnish), covers the country's entire history of seafaring, with special emphasis on the local region and on the Finnish navy. The rural culture of the archipelago nearby also features strongly. What most visitors will find memorable is the museum's extensive collection of real ships, many of which are moored in the river. They include the beautiful three-masted full-rigger *Suomen Joutsen*, just over a century old, and the barque *Signy*, described as 'the last wooden three-masted sail-powered trading vessel in the world'. There are also a couple of warships, a lovely little steamship, and Pikkuföri (little ferry), which, in the summer months, provides the nicest way to get to Forum Marinum from the city centre. The centre also has a shop and café.
Linnankatu 72, 20100 Turku.
Tel: (02) 282 9511;
www.forum-marinum.fi/english.
Open: summer daily, winter Tue–Sun.
Bus 1 from Market Sq and passenger harbour.

Luostarinmäki Handicrafts Museum

The Luostarinmäki Handicrafts Museum owes its existence to its location atop a hill south of the river.

This area escaped the great fire of 1827 and outwardly has remained much as it has been for centuries. Today it encompasses around 30 workshops where pre-industrial crafts and trades are carried on. There are two shops and a café on site.

The museum can be easily reached if you take a small detour from the City Walk (see *pp74–5*). Just past the Rettig Palace, cross Hämeenkatu and go up the short street opposite; climb the steps beside the mouth of the tunnel and continue up through Vartiovuori Park.
Luostarinmäki, 20100 Turku.
Tel: (02) 262 0350; www.turku.fi.
Open: summer daily, winter Tue–Sun shorter hours. Admission charge.
Buses 3, 12, 18, 24, 30 from Market Sq.

Market Hall (Kauppahalli)

North of the river, the central district still revolves around the Market Square (Kauppatori) (*Mon–Sat 7am–2pm and mid-May–mid-Sept Mon–Sat 7am–2pm and Mon–Fri evening market*).
Nearby is the red-brick Market Hall (Kauppahalli), which houses around 50 shops and cafés.
Eerikinkatu 16, 20100 Turku.
Open: Mon–Sat.
Free admission.

Qwensel House

Qwensel House is a survivor of the great fire and provides a vivid picture of the life and surroundings of an upper-class Finnish family of the early 18th century. Attached to it is the

Pharmacy Museum, showing how pharmacists used to prepare their own drugs. An inner courtyard reveals a bakery, a carriage house and outhouses which were part of the lifestyle of the wealthy. In summer, a herbalist's shop and café are also open.
Läntinen Rantakatu 13, 20100 Turku. Tel: (0) 2 262 0280; www.turku.fi. Open: summer daily, winter Tue–Sun shorter hours. Admission charge.

Rettig Palace

Rettig Palace, located close to the river and not far from the cathedral, houses two museums, Aboa Vetus and Ars Nova, plus a café and shop.

Aboa Vetus means 'Old Turku' (in a mix of Swedish and Latin). The museum is built over a medieval block which was discovered quite accidentally,

during renovation work. Now 7m (23ft) below the ground, the remains give a real insight into life in the medieval city. Changing exhibitions focus on particular aspects of history.

Ars Nova – 'New Art' in Latin – is exactly what its name suggests. The permanent collection here includes over 500 works of 20th- and 21st-century artists, both Finnish and foreign. There are also special exhibitions.
Itäinen Rantakatu 4-6, 20700 Turku. Tel: (0) 2 250 0552; www.aboavetusarsnova. fi/site/index.php/en. Open: daily apart from Mondays in winter, a few days at Midsummer and Christmas/New Year. Admission charge.Buses 13, 30, 55.

Sibelius Museum

Sibelius Museum, a stone's throw from the cathedral, is focused on the

Turku Castle

The steeple of Turku Cathedral

composer Jean Sibelius, but there is a lot more to it. It houses a remarkable collection of over 1,400 musical instruments from all over the world, of which around 300 are on display. The Sibelius Room contains original manuscripts and personal items from the composer's life. The museum also hosts changing exhibitions and regular chamber concerts.
Piispankatu 17, 20500 Turku.
Tel: (0) 2 215 4494; www.
sibeliusmuseum.abo.fi/index_eng.php.
Open: Tue–Sun & Wed evenings.
Admission charge.
Buses 4, 28, 30, 50, 51, 53, 54.

Turku Castle

Even more than the cathedral, Turku Castle embodies the city's importance in the history of Finland. The Swedish influence over southern Finland was primarily established by three 'crusades' – expeditions with both religious and imperialist aims, between the 1150s and 1239. Each of these was followed by the establishment of a fortress, at Turku, Häme and Viipuri (now Vyborg in Russia), respectively.

The exact date of the castle's foundation is uncertain but is estimated to be around 1280. At the same time, the pre-existing trading site was developing into the town of Åbo/Turku. The castle was originally an island in the estuary but water levels were then several metres higher, and the channel around has long since been filled in.

The original groundplan was rectangular with four gates, along the lines of a Roman camp. Extensions were added at intervals, with the original citadel forming the centre of the main keep. This incorporated a royal suite which was frequently used by Swedish kings when visiting their Finnish dominion. The castle continued to play a strategic role for many centuries, being subject to at least nine sieges before 1700, though most were a result of internal conflict rather than foreign aggression.

With the development of firearms and artillery, medieval castles became harder to defend without extensive earthworks, which were duly added. In the 1550s, the upper keep was rebuilt to create the so-called Renaissance Suite, which became the seat of John, the first Duke of Finland. John ruled as Duke here for seven years and his Polish wife brought a notable Italian faction into his court, introducing the first Renaissance influence in Finland. The military significance of the castle later declined but, like other castles in Finland, its solid granite construction ensured that it was not demolished.

Today, exhibition areas within the castle give further insight into its history, and that of the city and the nation. There are displays of glass, porcelain tableware and jewellery, and many of the rooms are decorated and furnished in different period styles.

There is a museum shop in the main courtyard.

Linnankatu 80, 20100 Turku.
Tel: (0) 2 262 0300; www.turku.fi.
Open: summer daily, winter Tue–Sun shorter hours.
Admission charge.
Bus 1 from Market Sq.

Looking upriver from Achim Kühn's sculpture *Harmony*, near Varvintori Square

Walk: Turku city

A walk down the banks of River Aura is a great way to see Turku. It passes many of the main sights and takes in its most distinctive views. Above all, this walk links the two great monuments of the city, the cathedral and the castle. It is a linear walk – rivers do not usually flow in circles – but it is easy to get back to the starting point as frequent buses (line 1) run past the castle.

Time: 1 hour without any stops, but with so many sights en route it could take all day. Distance: 3.5km (2¼ miles).

Start from Kauppatori (Market Square). Leave by the southeast corner and walk one block down Kauppaiskatu, passing the Grand Hotel Börs, a fine example of Finnish art nouveau. Turn left on Linnankatu to reach the riverbank.

1 Tuomiokirkkosilta (Cathedral bridge)

Although the bridge itself is busy with traffic, the tree-lined river affords a more peaceful atmosphere. The first bridge here was probably built in the 14th century; the present structure dates from 1899.

Cross the bridge and bear left across the square below the cathedral. If you want to visit the Sibelius Museum, continue onto Piispankatu; the museum is about 50m (55yds) ahead.

2 Turku Cathedral

The visitors' entrance is at the west end, the point of first arrival, and admission to the cathedral is free. Both inside and outside, the cathedral gives a sense of great height. The tower is 101m (331ft) tall.

Circumnavigate the cathedral. Re-cross the main road, then follow the foot-and cycle-path down, passing the Old Great Square. Soon you will pass the Rettig Palace, home to the Aboa Vetus and Ars Nova museums. Cross the river again by the next bridge (Auransilta), then continue downstream.

3 Läntinen Rantakatu

In quick succession along this stretch of the riverbank you will pass the Pharmacy Museum and Qwensel House, and then the art nouveau Town Hall.

Cross back to the south bank on Teatterisilta (cycles and pedestrians only), cross the main road and go up the street opposite, bearing right to the Biological Museum. Optionally, continue straight down the riverbank.

4 Maartinsilta

This is the last bridge, and below it large ships are very much in evidence, from unmoving floating restaurants to cruise ships, and, just a little further down, commercial cargo vessels. *Continue downriver to the little ferry, or Föri, which shuttles to and fro all day long. Cross here and carry on down the north bank. Pass Varvintori Square, and then the first of the museum ships belonging to Forum Marinum, the barque Sigyn.*

5 Forum Marinum

The main buildings of Forum Marinum, Turku's maritime museum, are only reached after you've passed its great museum ships: *Sigyn*, followed by the

huge white *Suomen Joutsen*. However, at this stage of the walk you may be more interested in the excellent café. *Leave the riverbank to skirt part of the commercial port, following a wire fence to a railway level crossing. Beyond this is a road and pedestrian crossing and then a small footbridge leads into the castle grounds. Bear right to reach the entrance.*

6 Turku Castle

The castle itself appears suddenly and massively ahead as you enter the grounds. If there's time it's worth walking round outside before entering, to get a better feel for the scale of the whole. *Buses back to Kauppatori leave from Linnankatu.*

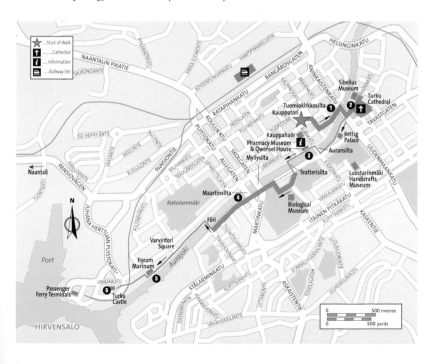

TURKU ENVIRONS
Naantali

Naantali is an exceptionally pretty and historic seaside town just 17km (10$^{1}/_{2}$ miles) from Turku. Its guest harbour is right in the heart of the old town, with its several streets of well-preserved wooden houses. Naantali has been a spa town since the 18th century, when the first visitors came to take the waters. Its ease of access and its many attractions for visitors mean that it can be very busy in the high season, when pre-booking for restaurants and accommodation is strongly advised. Those who prefer a quiet life will find it easier to appreciate its charms at other times of the year.

Not surprisingly, there is no lack of galleries and craft shops in the Old Town and you can find them by simply wandering around the historic streets. However, many of them (but fortunately not all) are open only in the summer season.

The town was founded in 1443 and, for several centuries, was the site of a convent. All that remains of the convent today is the beautiful Convent Church, which still dominates the view across the harbour. The nave dates from the mid-15th century, while the baroque belfry was added in 1797 (*tel: (0) 2 437 5420*). *Naantali Tourist Service.*
Tel: (0) 2 435 9860;
www.naantalinmatkailu.fi/eng

You can cycle to Naantali from Turku and the route is well signposted in both directions. Alternatively, bus numbers

MOOMINS

Moomins are the creation of the Helsinki-born author Tove Jansson (1914–2001). Jansson produced numerous books for adults, illustrations and other works, but her worldwide reputation rests mostly on her Moomin books. First published between 1949 and 1970, they have now been translated into over 30 languages. Moomins are small creatures that live in a secluded valley deep in the Finnish forests and hibernate through the winters. Apart from Naantali's Moominworld, there is a permanent Moominvalley exhibition in Tampere Art Museum.

11, 110 and 111 leave every 15 minutes from the Market Square.

In the summer, you can get there on the MS *Ukkopekka*, the last steamship that still regularly plies Finland's coastal waters. The cruise, lasting a little under two hours, is a great introduction to the magical Turku archipelago. Dishes made of locally caught fish are popular items on the buffet menu.
Bus 1 from Market Sq.
Linnankatu 38, 20100 Turku.
Tel: (0) 2 515 3300; www.ukkopekka.fi

Naantali Museum

Just a couple of blocks from the harbour is Naantali Museum, the best place to learn about the history of the town. The museum occupies two fine old houses. The main historical exhibition is in House Humppi, while across the street House Hilolola has rooms furnished to reflect the lifestyle of a bourgeois family in 19th-century Naantali. There is also a craft workshop

in the courtyard, and a museum shop.
*Katinhäntä 1 & Mannerheiminkatu 21.
Tel: (0) 2 434 5321. Open: mid-May–
end Aug Tue–Sun. Admission charge.*

Naantali Spa Hotel

The town's long spa tradition continues
today at the five-star Naantali Spa
Hotel. Spa facilities include sauna, pool
and aqua therapies, and are available
to non-residents.
*Matkailijantie 2, 21100 Naantali.
Tel: (0) 2 445 5800;
www.naantalispa.fi/english/index.html*

Kultaranta

On the other side of Naantali Bay is
Kultaranta, the official summer

residence of the President of Finland.
The castle-like granite edifice is not
open to the public (even Presidents
need their privacy) but the surrounding
gardens can be visited on a guided tour.
They include a grand formal garden
and a wild woodland area. In summer
there are daily tours (except Mondays).
Buses pick you up from the Spa Hotel
and Maariankatu, near the harbour. It
is best to book beforehand through the
Naantali Tourist Service. Group tours
can be arranged at other times.
Tel: (0) 2 435 9800.

Kailo

The island of Kailo, linked by a
causeway to the shore just beyond the

Historic wooden houses in Naantali

Enjoying a ferry ride in the Turku Archipelago

harbour, is home to **Moominworld**, 'a fairytale that you can step right into'. Among the trees you will find many of the characters from the Moomin stories; you can visit their homes, and see dramatisations of their stories at Theatre Emma. Children can have their faces painted to look like their favourite character. There are also the Moomin Shop and Mamma's Donut Shop in the Old Town.

Special Moominbuses run from/to Turku.
Tel: (0) 2 511 1111;
www.muumimaailma.fi/englanti.
Open: summer daily. Admission charge.

Väski

Right next to the Moominworld causeway, boats leave regularly for Väski, an island a few kilometres away. It is an appealing mix of an adventure playground and fantasy role-playing games, which should appeal to slightly older children, and perhaps a lot of parents.

Kaivokatu 5, 21101 Naantali.
Tel: (0) 2 511 1188; www.vaski.fi.
Open: summer daily. Admission charge.

TURKU PLACE NAMES

The communities residing in the Archipelago are bilingual but Swedish is the first language of the majority. To maintain consistency, throughout this book the Finnish name of a location is always given first, but in the Archipelago it is usually the Swedish name that you will see or hear first – so Parainen is mostly called Pargas, and so on.

THE TURKU ARCHIPELAGO

The Turku Archipelago (Finnish Turun Saaristo; Swedish Åbo Skargård) is variously credited with anything from twenty to forty thousand islands, depending on how many reefs and skerries are included. In any case, the number changes all the time as Baltic tides alternately cover and expose low-lying rocks, and as the land is still rising from the sea, more islands appear over time.

The Archipelago is a region of exceptional beauty, where the usual Finnish features of rock, trees and water are woven into an ever-changing tapestry. While some of the closer islands are now linked to the mainland by bridges, the heart of the Archipelago is accessible only by boat. For those with their own yachts there are small, friendly guest harbours on all the main islands. For the rest there are ferries.

It has been said that the longer you spend in the Archipelago, the more there is to see. It is, above all, a place to slow down, to linger, to look and to listen. If you pick the right spot – which is not hard to do – the only sounds you will hear will be the breeze in the trees or waves lapping against the shoreline.

A ring of larger islands is clearly evident on the map and is accessible by the usual touring routes (*see pp82–3*). To the south of these is the Archipelago National Park, made up of thousands of

Southwest Finland and the west coast

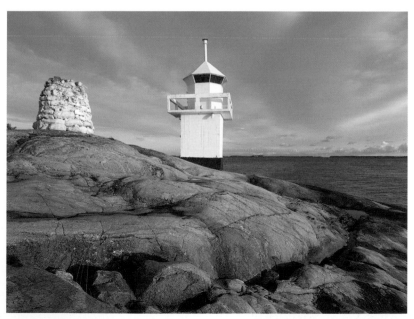

Heponiemi lighthouse

islands covering an area of 500sq km (193sq miles). Many of these are little more than bare rocks, but there are also some which have surprisingly rich forests, summer grazing and beautiful meadows, still managed in a traditional way. On the larger islands there may be moose in the forests. The seas support diminishing numbers of the Baltic ringed seal, while the grey seal population is steadily rising.

The standard archipelago trail is a circuit of around 200km (124 miles), starting and finishing in Turku. It is possible to drive through the whole circuit in a day, but you would be missing out on a lot. If a day is all you have, it is better to take the shorter Rymättylä–Nauvo–Parainen route. This will also leave you with some time to stop in the villages or wander along the coast.

The low-lying archipelago, with its quiet roads, is also ideal for cycling. Turku TouRing arranges complete packages, including accommodation and bike hire as required (*available from June–mid-Aug*).

There are no big 'attractions' in the archipelago, and that in itself is the attraction. It almost seems invidious to single out any one site for special attention, but a few recommendations will probably be useful, at least as starting points.

Parainen (Pargas)

Parainen (Pargas) is the only town in the archipelago; indeed the municipality is a mini-archipelago in its

MIDSUMMER POLE

In a land with such contrasting seasons, it is not surprising that midsummer is a particularly significant time. Although the midnight sun is only seen north of the Arctic Circle, it does not get properly dark at midsummer even in the south. It is also a time of great fertility and renewal, and celebration. This often takes the form of staying up all night and drinking lots of beer, but older traditions survive, and are particularly strong in the rural southwest. Notable among these is the decoration of the midsummer pole, which in maritime areas often resembles a ship's mast, with flowers and fruit, which then remain throughout the year.

own right. Water is never very far away and there is a guest harbour right in the centre of the town.

It is curious, then, that one of its main claims to fame is its limestone quarry, worked ever since the 14th century and now over 100m (328ft) deep – the deepest in Finland. Its floor is well below sea level. There is an impressive view of the quarry from the **Pargas Industrial Museum** at the intersection of Skräbbölevägen and Brunnsvägen (*tel: (0) 2 458 1452, (0) 50 596 2112; open: summer Sat–Sun*).

The old quarter, with its wooden houses and granite church, parts of which date back to the 14th century, is also worth a visit.

Nauvo (Nagu)

Nauvo (Nagu) is also an archipelago in itself, encompassing two main islands,

Lillandet and Storlandet, and around 3,000 smaller islands and skerries. Nauvo village, with its fine 15th-century church and dwellings scattered among tall pine trees, is a good place to stay while exploring the area. There is, at least in summer, a range of accommodation and places to eat. Several handicraft stalls can also be found. Here too you can arrange fishing trips, canoe excursions or cruises. Ferries (*summer only*) run to Hanka in **Rymättylä**, calling at the island of **Själö** (**Seili**), a former leper colony, which has a pretty wooden church.

Korppoo (Korpo)

Korppoo (Korpo) is at the heart of the Archipelago. Only 10 per cent of the municipality is land; the rest is water, extending a long way south from the largest island, **Kyrkland**, and taking in a large section of the **Archipelago National Park** (*boat trips into the park can be arranged*).

Korppoo village is a dispersed sort of place, but it has a good range of services. The guest harbour is the best place to look for a restaurant. The centre of the village is somewhat reminiscent of an English village green. It is dominated by a grey stone church dating from the late 14th century (*open: May–July Sat–Sun afternoons*).

An unusual attraction a few kilometres away is the Rumar lookout tower, which offers great views of the outer Archipelago, especially of the national park.

Korpoström Archipelago Centre

A few kilometres to the south is Korpoström Archipelago Centre, its new buildings harmonising well with traditional styles. It holds seminars and lectures and acts as a social centre, but its main importance to the visitor is its permanent exhibition displaying facets of life in the Archipelago, past and present. *Tel: (0) 2 463 1701; www. skargardscentret.fi. It is also home to Café-Restaurant Korpoströmmingen (tel: (0) 40 724 3524).*

Rymättylä (Rimito)

Rymättylä (Rimito) is a district of rich soils, noted for the growing of potatoes, vegetables and flowers. The produce is often sold on the roadside. Fishing is also of great importance traditionally.

Not far from the ferry pier at **Hanka** you can take a short walk (green-topped poles mark the route) to a large collection of Bronze Age burial mounds. Rymättylä is hillier than most of the islands, something that will be evident to anybody cycling through it, but it does mean there are some good viewing points.

About 2km (1¼ miles) from the Hanka pier is the start of the path to **Karhuvuori**, or 'bear mountain', though it is not quite a mountain even by British standards (nor are you likely to meet any bears). It is, however, a great lookout point, which served as an observation post in World War II.

Drive or cycle: Turku Archipelago

This circuit can only be completed in summer as some of the ferries are seasonal. At other times you can get from Parainen to Korppoo but will have to backtrack from there. Many (but not all) restaurants and places to stay are also seasonal. For much of the way through the islands the motoring and cycling routes are the same, but on the mainland there are separate cycle tracks most of the way that avoid the busier roads. Many of the ferries (the yellow ones) are free.

Time: for cyclists 4–5 days, for drivers 2 days.

The map shows both routes and drivers will also find the route well signposted. The following detailed description is mainly for cyclists.

1 Parainen (Pargas)

Parainen is the largest settlement in the archipelago. Its attractions include a pleasant harbour and wooden houses around a granite church.
Continue along quiet roads, passing the quarry. Loop southward on unsealed roads before rejoining the highway for the approach to the first ferry. After this it's about 15km (9 1/2 miles) to Nauvo/Nagu village.

2 Nauvo (Nagu)

The village straggles past a medieval church, down to a sheltered harbour. It's all pretty lively in summer but for nine months of the year Nauvo can definitely be described as 'sleepy'.

Follow another unsealed road close to the north coast, rejoining the highway before the ferry to Korppoo/Korpo.

3 Korppoo (Korpo)

If time allows, it is well worth continuing the extra 3km (1 3/4 miles) into the village of Korppoo. Its medieval church is probably the finest in the Archipelago, with some notable medieval sculpture inside. Across from the church is an attractive manor house dating from 1803.
Continue along the highway for 6km (3 1/2 miles) to the turning for the Houtskär ferry. This crossing is longer and ferries are less frequent. Follow the main road to Mossala, taking in two shuttle ferries.

4 Mossala

The crossing from Mossala to Iniö is the longest on the route, taking almost an hour, but has wonderful views.

Check ferry times carefully as there are only about four crossings each day. Continue north across Iniö, with another ferry hop, to Jumo/Kannvik and the crossing to Heponiemi.

5 Heponiemi

Heponiemi is on the island of Kustavi. Overlooking the ferry terminal is the Old Coastguard Station (1961), now a B&B and café. The upper floors have unrivalled views of the archipelago. *Head north to join highway 192. At Taivassalo turn right to Hakkenpää for the crossing to Teersalo.*

6 Hakkenpää–Teersalo

Make sure you catch the right departure, as this ferry serves several destinations and you could find yourself back on Iniö! Teersalo is on the island of Livonsaari but it's joined to the mainland by a bridge. *Follow road 1931 then turn right on tracks alongside the 1930 to Merimasku. Turn left along the busy 189, but after a bridge the lanes and cycletracks weave pleasantly into Naantali.*

7 Naantali

After the archipelago, the summer bustle of Naantali may come as a bit of a shock, but it is a beautiful seaside town, with origins dating back to 1443, and home to the luxury Naantali Spa Hotel. *Follow the shoreline (past the bridge to Moominworld) and then follow the well-signposted cycle tracks and lanes to Turku.*

Drive or cycle: Turku Archipelago

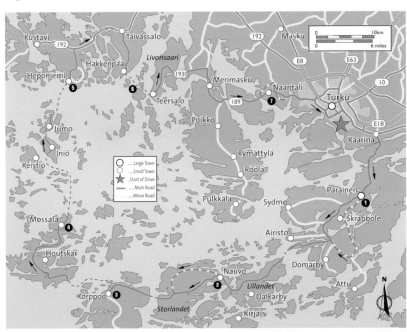

Cycling in Finland

In many ways Finland is ideal for cycling, whether you are a hardened mile-eater or an occasional rider. Provision for cycling is generally excellent, with most towns and cities possessing a network of routes that will make British riders green with envy. Roads are quiet in the countryside – certainly by British standards – and Finnish drivers are generally respectful of two-wheeled traffic.

A cyclist in Helsinki

Even for those who are not regular cyclists, the terrain is encouraging, with few climbs that are either long or steep, and almost none that are both. It is important to remember, though, that the distances between towns, especially in the north, are considerable. Ruka and Kuusamo, which on a general map may appear to be next to each other, are 20km (12^1/$_2$ miles) apart; Kuusamo to Oulu is a distance of over 200km (124 miles).

Major tours in the north are best left to the seasoned cycle-tourist, but those in the south, where places to stop are much closer together, are better for the amateur. Routes like the Turku Archipelago (*see pp82–3,154*) or The King's Road (*see pp106–109*) cover gentle terrain with plenty of stopping places, so daily distances can normally be kept to a manageable 40 or 50km (25 or 30 miles). Of course you will need to carry some belongings with you – changes of clothes and toiletries, and no doubt a camera – but if you pack carefully the weight should only be a few kilos. While this can fit in a small rucksack, it is better to carry it in a pannier or saddlebag. Or you can book with a tour operator who will transport your luggage for you.

For hardy souls there are several possibilities. One recommended circuit is in the lake country west of Jyväskylä: four days, with the longest stretch 45km (28 miles), though some parts are quite hilly. Another route comprises a 330km (205-mile) circuit around Lake Saimaa, for which you will have to plan for seven or eight days. For more suggestions, the Finnish Tourist Board publishes a brochure dedicated to cycling, and there are comprehensive cycling pages on their website: *www.visitfinland.com* and search for 'cycling'.

It is worth remembering that most Finnish trains carry bikes, so you don't need to limit yourself to circular routes. Bikes cannot be carried on Pendolino trains, and on the InterCity services they should be booked in advance.

If you don't fancy a multi-day tour there are lots of day rides on offer. Bikes can be hired in most towns: local tourist information centres can advise on availability and suitable routes.

Mountain-bike enthusiasts will be happy to learn that 'every man's right' applies to bikes too. You can cycle freely in the countryside, except in gardens, in the immediate vicinity of people's homes, and in fields and plantations which could easily be damaged.' However, shooting off into the wilds at random is not

A cyclist tours the Turku Archipelago

recommended as you could fall foul of rocks, swamps or dense forest. Local tourist information centres can advise on good routes.

Many Finns cycle all the year round, even in temperatures of −20°C (−4°F) or below, but this may have limited appeal to visitors! The temperature itself is not too much of a problem, if you are dressed appropriately, but riding over icy surfaces is not everyone's cup of tea.

FISKARI

To the south and west of Helsinki, in the direction of Hanko – Finland's southernmost town – a number of iron-working villages developed in the 17th century. The best known of these is Fiskari, though it is the Swedish version of the name that is more likely to ring a bell, as it is the home of Fiskars, a company known internationally as producers of high-quality scissors, knives, etc.

Trains between Turku and Helsinki stop at Karjaa, about 11km (7 miles) from Fiskari. Buses to Fiskari from here are not very frequent, so it may be necessary to take a taxi.

The village is essentially strung along a reach of the River Fiskari, between two sets of rapids. The area that visitors see first consists of a whole series of carefully preserved buildings which house a range of workshops and galleries. Although from the outside it may look like an open-air museum, Fiskari is a thriving centre of art and design, much of it contemporary.

Fiskari is one of a number of ironworks villages that were established in the region in the early 17th century. In addition to ore, they had water power (needed for the crushing of the ore) and forests to provide fuel in the form of charcoal. A crushing mill was established by the lower rapids in 1649, with a blast furnace on the opposite bank. With the progress of the industrial revolution, the production of iron and subsequently steel moved to increasingly larger plants, fuelled by coal rather than charcoal. The owners

Fiskari

took the far-sighted decision to convert from production to metalworking, and a cutlery mill was founded in the 1830s with the help of craftsmen from Sheffield (UK).

Bianco Blu

Facing the forge is the Bianco Blu glass-blowing workshop.
Tel: (0) 50 562 3195; www.biancoblu.fi.
Open: June–Aug & Dec daily; rest of year Mon–Sat.

Clock tower

The focal point of the village is the clock tower building. This includes an exhibition space, a very pleasant café and a gallery showcasing local art and craft work. These are operated by Onoma, the local artisans', designers' and artists' cooperative.
Tel: (0) 19 277 7500; www.onoma.org.
Open: summer daily, winter Tue–Sun.

There are workshops and shops throughout the village, and visitors can spend endless time just wandering around.

Forge

Given the history of the place, it seems appropriate to start with the forge, which is located across the first bridge. Here you can see traditional blacksmithing skills being practised, though there is a modern element in the design of many of the products.
Tel: (0) 50 590 2797.
Open: summer daily.

Glasswork on display in the old granary

Old granary

On the way to the forge you pass the old granary, now home to changing exhibitions of local contemporary art and design. The work itself may inspire anything from adoration to ridicule, but it is a great space to view it. It is worth taking a close look at the exterior walls of the granary and the nearby mill, as their blackish 'slag' bricks are like art objects themselves.

UUSIKAUPUNKI

To describe a place as pleasant may seem like damning it with faint praise, but in the case of Uusikaupunki, it is hard to think of a better word. Pleasant is exactly what it is, but there's nothing faint about this praise. It has much of the charm of places like Naantali, but without the mega-attractions and sometimes excessive crowds, making it much more relaxing for a summer visit. It has an interesting church and a couple of worthwhile museums, but in many ways it is a place to just relax, take a leisurely walk through the surrounding countryside or along the shore, and to watch the comings and

Uusikaupunki harbour

goings at the marina from a waterfront bar or restaurant.

The name means 'new town', and, like most places with similar names, it is far from new. It was founded in 1617 and it played host to the signing of the Treaty of Uusikaupunki in 1721.
Tourist Information. Tel: (0) 2 8451 5443; www.uusikaupunki.com

Automobile Museum, Saab Collection and Garage Museum
Car-lovers will enjoy these comprehensively self-explanatory collections.
Autotehtaankatu 14. Tel: (0) 20 484 8068. Open: daily. Admission charge.

BONK Centre
British visitors will hardly be able to resist a smile at the name of the BONK Centre, an idiosyncratic and unique collection of bizarre devices.
Siltakatu 2. Tel: (0) 2 841 8404; www.bonkcentre.fi.
Open: summer daily, rest of the year Mon–Fri. Admission charge.

Old Church
The oldest building in town is the Old Church, dating back to 1629, and noted for its barrel-vaulted ceiling, decorated with stars.
Tel: (0) 2 840 4505. Open: summer daily. Free admission.

RAUMA
The Old Town of Rauma is one of Finland's five World Heritage Sites. It is the largest area of wooden houses in the Nordic countries. Covering an area of 28 hectares (69 acres) and including

more than 600 buildings, it is an impressive and colourful collection. However, what is attractive about Vanha Rauma (its Finnish name) is that it is not a museum, preserved in aspic, but a real, living community. This also means that, unlike many of Finland's historic sites, it doesn't turn into a ghost town at the end of August. You can visit Rauma at any time of the year, and it might even be better off-season, as the locals then outnumber tourists.

The town was founded in 1442, beginning as a trading centre attached to a Franciscan monastery. Its inhabitants (along with those of several other towns) were forcibly evicted in 1550 to populate the new town of Helsinki, and were not allowed to return until 1557. Rauma's great tradition of lace-making was brought back by far-travelled seamen. At its height, when lace bonnets were worn across Europe, many hundreds of people worked in lace production. The industry has enjoyed a revival and it is reckoned that there are around 150 practitioners, professional and amateur, in Rauma today. Several studios can be seen while walking around the Old Town, and on summer days there are also open-air demonstrations.

A customs barrier was erected around the town in the 17th century, limiting its growth. Although the rising land meant that the centre of the port moved away from the Old Town, people continued to live here. The closing decades of the sailing-ship era in the late 19th century were an era of great prosperity. There was much renovation at this time, though behind the façades many buildings have elements from a century or more earlier.

Church of the Holy Cross

On the edge of the Old Town is the Church of the Holy Cross (Pyhän Ristin Kirkko). This was built in the late 15th/early 16th century to serve a Franciscan monastery in the area. The exact date seems uncertain but it is thought to have been completed in 1512. The monastery was disbanded in 1538 during the Reformation. The existing parish church was destroyed by fire in 1640, and the Church of the Holy Cross became the Lutheran parish church. The west tower was added in 1816, using stones from the ruins of the Church of the Holy Trinity. The interior walls and ceiling feature

The Old Town Hall in Rauma

Pori, from the Kokemäenjoki River

medieval paintings. A notable feature is the ornate pulpit, carved in Germany in 1625. There is also a massive 24-branched chandelier dating from 1648. *Open: daily May–Sept. Free admission.*

House Kirsti

This is the tiny home of a humble seaman, with just two rooms, and is simply furnished. The house dates from the 18th century, but is furnished as it would have been a little over 100 years ago.
Pohjankatu 3. Tel: (0) 2 834 3529; www.rauma.fi/museo. Open: summer daily. Admission charge. Free for children. The same ticket also covers the following two museums.

House Marela

This house is part of the Rauma Museum and represents a typical home of a wealthy ship-owning family. It is decorated and furnished in late 19th-century style.
Kauppakatu 24. Tel: (0) 2 834 3528; www.rauma.fi/museo. Open: summer daily, rest of the year Tue–Sun. Admission charge. Free for children.

Market Square (Kauppatori)

The lively Market Square (Kauppatori) in the centre of Vanha Rauma is dominated by the Old Town Hall, dating from 1776, which now houses the **Rauma Museum**. This documents the history of seafaring as well as the lace industry.
Kauppakatu 13, 26100 Rauma. Tel: (0) 2 834 3532; www.rauma.fi/museo. Open: summer daily, rest of the year Tue–Sun. Admission charge. Free for children.

PORI

The coastline around Pori is sometimes called the Finnish Riviera, which is not necessarily flattering to either France or Finland. The Bothnia shores do not have swanky resorts, just fine beaches and a necklace of offshore islands.

The town of Pori has one great claim to fame: the jazz festival, one of Finland's major festivals, held around the third week of July. As you would expect, the town gets very busy around this time and is best avoided unless you are there for the jazz.

Founded in 1558, the city and its surroundings still have strong industrial and sea-trading links, but it is now also a major university town. The city centre has some fine neoclassical buildings, including the **Old Courthouse**, designed by C L Engel, which houses the Tourist Office, and the **Central Church**, dating from 1863, with its unusual open-work spire and art nouveau interior (*tel: (0) 2 633 2955; open: daily. Free admission*).

Pori Art Museum

Pori Art Museum is one of Finland's leading art museums, with constantly changing exhibitions. It also has a café and shop.

Eteläranta, 28100 Pori. Tel: (0) 2 621 1080; www.pori.fi/art/satakunta/pori. eng. Open: Tue–Sun. Admission charge. Free guided tours available on Wed evenings.

KIRJURINLUOTO

Just a short walk from the centre is the island of Kirjurinluoto, the main setting for Pori's annual summer jazz festival. At other times it is a pleasant green

Kite-surfers at Yyteri beach

oasis with a sandy beach, playgrounds and a restaurant.

YYTERI

At Yyteri, about 15km (9^1/$_2$ miles) north of Pori, they'll tell you they have the best beach in Finland, and they could well be right. It is a grand crescent of fine white sand backed by pine-covered dunes. It also boasts a surf centre, and there aren't too many of those in Finland. The enclosed waters of the Gulf of Bothnia do not, of course, generate big waves, so the focus here is on windsurfing and kite-surfing. Towed by something more like a parachute than a kite, surfers can reach speeds of more than 60kph (37mph), and even become spectacularly airborne. It is a great spectator sport, especially when seen back-lit by the setting sun.

You can also try windsurfing, thanks to **Yyteri Surfcenter** (*on the beach next to the Spa Hotel; tel: (0) 50 512 1366; open: May–Oct*).

There are lots of other activities too, like hiking and kayaking. There is a golf course and the very unusual Frisbee Golf. And there is a nudist beach, well screened by the dunes.

VAASA

Vaasa (Vasa) is a city of great historic significance, but its ancient atmosphere is not exactly overwhelming. Even the Old Town, about 2km (1 mile) from the modern centre, is unremarkable. However, it is supposed to be the sunniest part of Finland, and there are several places of interest nearby, for which Vaasa makes an excellent base.

The area to the southwest is the main attraction, and is perfectly suited to a leisurely day's exploration, ideally by bike.

Start by heading across the bridge to the island of Vaskiluoto (Vasklot), home to the main commercial harbour and the cheery little amusement park of Wasalandia. Continue into tranquil rural surroundings, through Sundom, to the village of Sulva (Solf). This is an attractive little place, with a lot of charming wooden houses and well-tended gardens, while tucked away just off the road is Stundars, one of Finland's best open-air museums.

Stundars

It began as the brainchild of the local elementary school teacher, Gunnar Rosenholm, who encouraged many villagers to join in his grand project. The site now features around 60 buildings which have been relocated from the surrounding region, assembled and furnished to give a comprehensive picture of rural life around a century ago. In summer, Stundars is full of life, with demonstrations of all kinds of traditional skills and crafts. There are art studios, a craft shop and café. *Stundarsvägen 5, FIN-65450 Sulva. Tel: (0) 6 344 2200; www.stundars.fi. Open: summer daily, rest of the year for groups by appointment. Admission charge.*

The longest bridge in Finland, Raippaluoto (Replot)

Söderfjärden

Just to the west is Söderfjärden, one of Finland's most striking geological sites. A roughly circular depression, it has been identified as the remnant of a meteorite impact around 550 million years ago. The floor of the depression used to be swampy. It has now been drained, yielding rich farmland, which contrasts sharply with the stony, forested rim. It is also a very important area for migratory birds, notably cranes.

The best view is from the air (so keep a good lookout if you happen to fly in or out of Vaasa), but you can get a pretty fair impression from several points around the rim.

It is best to head for Öjberget, the highest point, following the ski slope signs – yes, there is a ski slope on a hill just over 50m (164ft) high. *www.vasa.abo.fi/luc/soderfjarden/en/ index.htm*

Raippaluoto (Replot)

About 15km (9 miles) north of Vaasa is the island of Raippaluoto (Replot), along with a gaggle of smaller islands. It has been linked to the mainland by a bridge since 1997. The bridge, just over a kilometre (²/₃ mile) long, is the longest in Finland and a minor attraction in itself. Despite the new ease of access, Raippaluoto and its archipelago are generally peaceful.

Walk: Rauma Old Town

You can't go wrong just wandering at random around the fascinating streets of Vanha Rauma, but to be sure of taking in all the significant features, the following itinerary is suggested. The walk is less than 2km (1¹/4 miles) long, so you could get around in half an hour, but you should allow at least 3 hours to explore all the sights.

The walk starts from the Kauppatori. Leave the square at the northwest corner (far left if you stand with your back to the Old Town Hall), and follow the street to a small bridge.

1 Kirkkosilta

Kirkkosilta mean 'Church Bridge' and the Church of the Holy Cross rises just beyond. The stream below is called the Raumanjoki, or Rauma River.

Turn left, staying on the left (south) bank of the stream and walk down Vähäkoulokatu. Follow this, with a slight dogleg crossing another street, then turn left on Lansikatu and follow this down to its end. Turn left onto Kuninkaankatu.

2 Kuninkaankatu

This is the principal thoroughfare of the Old Town, and its shops sell all kinds of everyday goods as well as crafts and souvenirs. There are several pleasant cafés too.

Take the first right on Pappilankatu. Where it seems to end, go left, and after 20m (22yds) go right. At the next 'end' turn right and then take the first left – this is still Pappilankatu, though it opens almost immediately into Helsingintori.

3 Helsingintori (Helsinki Square)

Legend has it that when the Swedish King, Gustav Vasa, decided to found Helsinki, he ordered a number of Rauma's inhabitants to move there, and this is where they gathered before departure. It is also home to a fine statue of a lace-maker, sculpted in 1976 by Kauko Räike.

Leave the square and continue in the direction you were walking when you turned into the square – and, yes, it's still Pappilankatu! Take the first left into Isomalminkatu. At its end go left on Isopoikkikatu. Where this ends, turn right on Eteläpitkäkatu and follow this until it opens out into a large square.

4 Holy Trinity Church

In its centre are the ruins of the Holy Trinity Church, built in the 15th century

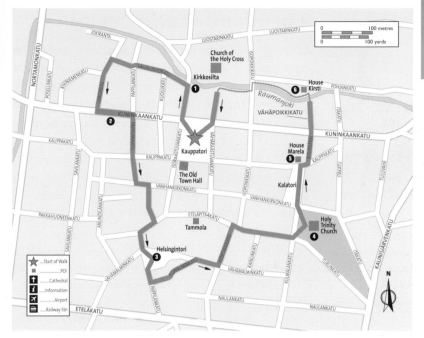

and destroyed by fire in 1640. There is not much left to see, just the base of the main walls, but you can't fail to be impressed by the sheer mass of some of the granite blocks.

Turn left and continue past the modern Hotel Kalatori. Kalatori itself is the smaller cobbled square ahead.

5 House Marela

Kalatori is the former fish market, once very important in this maritime town. At the end of the square is House Marela, one of the finest houses in town. Its ornately decorated façade is matched by impressive panelling and ceramic stoves on the inside.

Turn right, then first left on Kitukränn (said to be the narrowest street in

Finland). Continue straight across into the more normally proportioned Vähäpoikkikatu. At the end cross a small bridge.

6 House Kirsti

House Kirsti is a much more humble dwelling; even without entering, just by glancing into the courtyard you get a glimpse of a simple life. The narrow path, which you follow next, is also particularly redolent of Rauma's past.

Turn left along a narrow path beside the stream and soon the Church of the Holy Cross appears again. Cross the next bridge and continue on the left bank of the stream. Bear left when opposite the church, and soon you're back in the Kauppatori.

The Åland Islands

Both physically and culturally, the Åland Archipelago represents a bridge between Finland and Sweden. The islands, which are overwhelmingly Swedish-speaking, were invaded by the Russians in 1808 and incorporated into the Grand Duchy of Finland by the Treaty of Frederikshamn the following year. The islands were attacked and partly taken over by British and French forces during the Crimean War. In subsequent negotiations they were declared a demilitarised zone. Despite this, the islands saw fighting in 1918 during the Finnish Civil War.

Subsequently the 'Åland question' was taken to the League of Nations. Finnish sovereignty was confirmed, but with a high degree of autonomy and guarantees protecting language, culture and customs. The islands were largely peaceful during World War II: some fortifications were constructed but were demolished immediately after the war.

After several revisions to the Åland Autonomy Act, the islands now have their own flag, and issue their own stamps. Far more are produced than needed locally, as they are extremely popular with collectors.

The current population is around 26,500, spread over 150 of the archipelago's total of around 6,500 islands. The main island represents around two-thirds of the total land area. It is also home to the bulk of the people, with over 10,000 living in Mariehamn, the only town. The electorate votes for a 30-seat Parliament which has tax-raising powers and

control over a wide range of issues. The Finnish President has a strictly limited veto power over laws passed by the Åland Parliament. You can see parallels with British offshore islands like the Isle of Man or the Channel Islands, but each is subtly different.

Physically, the Åland archipelago resembles many of the other skeins of islands off the shores of Finland, but on a larger scale. The main island is by far the largest in Finland. As the land continues to rise following the last ice age, the Åland and Turku archipelagos will in the distant future become a land bridge between Sweden and Finland, and the Gulf of Bothnia will become a lake.

Like the other offshore islands, the Åland islands are generally low-lying, with largely rocky shores of reddish granite. The interior landscapes are a mix of cultivated land and woodland, with a higher proportion of broad-leaved trees than is usual in Finland.

Åland is well connected to both Finland and Sweden by ferry and air services. The main point of arrival is Mariehamn, though ferries also link Grisslehamn in Sweden with the western Åland island of Eckerö. Within the islands there are now many bridges and causeways, and local ferries, some of which carry only bikes and pedestrians.

Swedish is the only official language on Åland; road and street signs are monolingual, and therefore, unlike elsewhere in this book, Swedish forms are used in these pages too.

Mariehamn

Mariehamn is an attractive, spacious town, noted for its wide tree-lined streets, sitting on a strip of land around 1km (²/₃ mile) wide, which means that nowhere is more than a few minutes' walk from one of the harbours. The western harbour, **Västra Hamnen**, is where ferries from Sweden and Finland dock. Both harbours have yacht marinas, the eastern one, **Östra Hamnen**, being the larger, with about 300 berths. Östra

Västra Hamnen, Mariehamn, with the *Pommern* towering behind

Hamnen is the focal point of the town. It is easy to get around on foot, but there is also a free bus service that tours the town every half hour.

Åland Museum & Åland Art Museum

The Åland Museum, regarded as Åland's national museum, was declared European Museum of the Year in 1982. It provides a wide-ranging picture of the natural and human history of Åland from prehistoric times to the present day. The presentation is unusual and imaginative. Under the same roof is the Åland Art Museum, its permanent exhibition concentrating on visual arts from or about the islands. *Stadshusparken, AX-22100 Mariehamn. Tel: (0) 18 25 000; www.aland-museum.aland.fi. Open: summer daily, rest of the year Tue–Sun. Admission charge.*

Ålands Sjöfartsmuseum (Maritime Museum)

You can buy a combined ticket to visit the Maritime Museum and the adjacent *Pommern*. It originated with the personal collection of Captain Carl Holmqvist of Mariehamn, and focuses on the sailing-ship era, with many paintings and models of ships and a collection of figureheads. There is also a small shop. *PB 98, AX-22101 Mariehamn. Tel: (0) 18 19 930; www.sjofartsmuseum.aland.fi. Open: daily, winter shorter hours. Admission charge.*

Pommern

Ålander Gustaf Erikson is reckoned to have owned the biggest sailing-ship fleet in the world. In 1923, he acquired the four-masted barque *Pommern*, built at Glasgow in 1903 for a German company. Moored at the northern end of Västra Hamnen, with its masts towering over the quay, *Pommern* is one of the last great sailing ships.

There are no regular guided tours but plenty of posted information (English included). You can also rent an audio guide.

Museifartyget POMMERN, AX-22101 Mariehamn. Tel: (0) 18 531 421; www.pommern.aland.fi/welcome.htm. Open: summer daily. Admission charge.

Sjökvarteret

Mariehamn's strong seafaring tradition fostered several prosperous shipowners. At the north end of Östra Hamnen is the Maritime Quarter, Sjökvarteret. While this does include a museum of shipbuilding, it is very much a living centre, including an active boatyard as well as a smithy and workshops for other crafts. A number of ships built here are based at the quay. The Schooner *Linden* offers day cruises in summer (*tel: (0) 0 181 2055; www.linden.aland.fi*). The Schooner *Nordboen* also offers day cruises as well as longer ones (*tel: (0) 40 721 3808; www.apalmersailing.aland.fi*).

There are plans to expand the facilities at Sjökvarteret, with a traditional marina under construction, and a rigging workshop in the pipeline.

Sjökvarteret, 22100 Mariehamn.
Tel: (0) 2 421 280;
http://personal.inet.fi/surf/sjokvarteret/english.html.
Maritime Quarter open: daily.
Museum open: summer daily, rest of the year Mon–Fri. Admission charge.

Åland is noted for its fantastic displays of wild flowers in spring. In the relatively mild climate of the archipelago, flowers may begin blooming towards the end of April, when much of Finland may still be

Meadows full of orchids are a feature of the Åland landscape

under snow. The displays probably peak towards the end part of May. Recommended places to see the flowers include the park of **Tullarn's Äng** in Mariehamn itself. A few kilometres from town, the little peninsula of Ramsholmen has a 1.5km (1-mile) hiking trail which is well known for its orchids. The peninsula and the adjacent bay of Torpfjärden are also great places for birdwatching.

Away from the relative bustle of Mariehamn, Åland is a mosaic of small communities. The generally flat terrain makes it ideal for exploring by bike, and the sheltered waters also lend themselves to canoe trips. Fishing is very popular here; so is hiking. The laid-back atmosphere lends itself to more relaxed pottering around rather than racing from one attraction to the next, but the archipelago has a few 'must-sees'.

Eckerö
Eckerö Mail & Customs House
In the early 19th century Åland was the western limit of the Russian empire and the town of Eckerö was the customs border with Sweden. The elegant Mail & Customs House was designed by the ubiquitous C L Engel and completed in 1828. It houses historical and art exhibitions and the old post office is a magnet for philatelists. There is also a fine café.
AX 22270 Eckerö. Tel: (0) 457 5244 000;
www.visitaland.com/en/post&tullhus.
Open: daily in summer.
Admission charge.

Sund
Bomarsund fortress
The evocative, ruined Bomarsund fortress in the district of Sund, in the northeast of the main island, was built by the Russians and begun in 1832. Its tall towers provide some of the best views over the archipelago.

A 5.5km ($3^1/_2$-mile) hiking trail loops through an attractive landscape, passing graves, the remains of the garrison hospital and many other remnants of the past. The trail passes along the tops of some cliffs whose bases were once washed by the waves, a reminder that the land here is still rising.

There is a small museum by the bridge, in an old pilot's cottage, portraying the history of Bomarsund.
Tel: (0) 18 44 032.
Open: summer daily.
Donations encouraged.

Kastelholm Castle
Kastelholm Castle, also in Sund is a fine medieval castle, now restored after several centuries of neglect. First established in the 14th century, it was the administrative centre for the whole of Åland district. One of the bailiffs of Kastelholm, Erik Johansson, was the father of the great Swedish King Gustav Vasa, who later imprisoned his brother here.
22520 Kastelholm. Tel: (0) 18 432 150.
Open: summer daily.
Admission charge.

Tampere

Tampere may be Finland's third largest city, but with only 200,000 people it is a tiny city by international standards. But there is always something going on here. It has a big-city 'buzz', and yet it is easy to escape to the lakes that surround it. It is also a very compact city, with nearly all the main attractions within walking distance.

Tampere owes its existence to its lakes, specifically to the Tammerkoski rapids that lie between them. The waters of Lake Näsijärvi, to the north, fall 18m (60ft) before entering Lake Pyhäjärvi. With the lakes serving an important role for transport, this became an important point for transshipment; the rapids also offered abundant water power, initially for grain milling, then for dyeing and paper-making.

The industrial revolution in Finland effectively began in Tampere when a Glasgow man, James Finlayson, founded a cotton mill in 1820, though it took several decades before industrialisation really took hold; an ironworks and a number of other textile mills were developed around the middle of the century.

Until the 1880s all factories used direct water power, supplemented by steam, but then Finlayson's began to generate electricity from the rapids, and by the 1930s there were four power stations spaced along the rapids.

Today most of the industries have ceased to operate or drastically changed their nature, but the power stations still provide electricity to the city. Several factory buildings have been turned to new uses, while the Tammerkoski rapids and their surroundings have been declared a national landscape.

Tampere has some unusual and attractive museums, notably the Lenin Museum and the Spy Museum. The former owes its existence to Finland's role as a refuge for many leading Bolsheviks in the period leading up to the Russian Revolution; the latter, to Finland's historic position as the only 'western' country apart from Norway to have a border with the Soviet Union.

In summer, another attraction is a cruise on the lakes.

Landmarks and orientation

The central area of Tampere is clearly defined by two lakes to the north and south. The Tammer River and rapids, slung between the lakes, are the main axis for the orientation of visitors; the key Tammerkoski area is towards the northern end. West of the river lies the large central square and shopping district, and a few blocks further west, the narrow linear park of Hameepuisto provides a green connection between the north and south shores. The railway station is a few blocks to the east of the river.

Finlayson complex

The Finlayson complex is a former textile mill which now houses museums, a cinema multiplex, artists' studios and bars, cafés, restaurants and galleries. It is easily reached by a pedestrian tunnel from the central square

Spy Museum

Lurking in the basement of the Finlayson complex, the Spy Museum is an entertaining place with displays of all kinds of weird and wonderful gadgets from the esoteric world of espionage. The great thing is that there are lots of opportunities to try them out yourself; you can even take a lie detector test. The 'Agent Tests' are all in English, and guided tours in English are also available. All the secrecy in the air, though, leads one inevitably to ask the question, "what are they not showing us?!"

Satakunnankatu 18, PL 76, 33101 Tampere. Tel: (0) 3 212 3007; www.vakoilumuseo.fi/englanti/index.htm. Open: daily, summer longer hours. Admission charge.

Lake cruises

Given Tampere's location between two lakes, there is a variety of lake cruises available in summer. One of the more interesting trips is from Tampere to Hämeenlinna. This takes most of the

The Tammerkoski River

day for a one-way trip, so most people return or proceed elsewhere by train. Hämeenlinna is on the main line between Tampere and Helsinki. (*Finnish Silverline, Laukontori 10 A, 33200 Tampere. Tel: (0) 3 212 4804; www.hopealinja.fi/sivut/english/ home.htm*)

There are many shorter cruises (some as short as 90 minutes) to choose from too, on both the Pyhäjärvi and Näsijärvi lakes.

Lenin Museum

The Lenin Museum is housed in the Workers' Hall, the venue of the first meeting between Lenin and Stalin in 1905. Following the collapse of the Soviet Union, it is now the only permanent Lenin museum in the world. The museum strives to present a balanced view rather than submerge the visitor in a tide of hagiographic propaganda. Today its focus has broadened slightly and the museum also pays attention to the history of the Soviet era and the complex relations between Finland and its giant eastern neighbour. It is also an important repository of documents that came to light in various archives following the collapse of the Soviet Union.
Hämeenpuisto 28, 3rd floor.
Tel: (0) 3 276 8100; www.lenin.fi.
Open: daily. Admission charge.
Book in advance for guided tours.

Moominvalley

Behind a somewhat secretive entrance

The Finlayson complex

on the lower floor of the Tampere City Library is Moominvalley, dedicated to the world of the Moomins created by Tove Jansson. It is essential viewing for Moomin fans, of course, but may also be of appeal for the unconverted. There is a lot of original material by Tove Jansson, and some charming models of scenes from the stories. Pride of place undoubtedly goes to the beautifully detailed Moominhouse, more than 2m (6^1/$_2$ft) tall. The static displays are backed up by multimedia shows, which are an attraction for children. There is also a small museum shop.
Hämeenpuisto 20. Tel: (0) 35 656 6578; www.tampere.fi/muumi/english.
Open: summer daily, rest of the year Tue–Sun. Admission charge.

Tallipiha Stable Yards

Behind the Finlayson complex are the Tallipiha Stable Yards, which formerly housed both the owner's (extensive) stable of horses and the staff employed to look after them. The owner's home used to be a palatial manor nearby, towards the rapids, which is now a restaurant.

The oldest of the Tallipiha buildings dates from the 1840s, though most of them belong to the later decades of the century. The architectural style is strongly Russian-influenced. The area, long neglected, has recently been restored to its former glory and now houses a range of craft workshops, gift shops and a café. In summer, there are rides around the area in a horse-drawn carriage. *Näsinpuisto.*
www.tampere.fi/tallipiha/english.
Open: summer daily, rest of the year Tue–Sun. Free admission.

Vapriikki

Tampere's principal museum centre is housed in a former engineering works. It is a good starting point for the visitor, as its central exhibition presents the history of the region from the last ice age to the present. Of more specific interest are the Finnish Hockey Hall of Fame, one of only five museums in the world specialising in the history of the sport, and the Shoe Museum. There is also a museum shop, and a café/restaurant.
Museum Centre Vapriikki, Veturiaukio 4, Tampella, 33101 Tampere.
Tel: (0) 35 656 6966;
www.tampere.fi/english/vapriikki.
Open: Tue–Sun, Wed evening.
Admission charge.

NÄSIJÄRVI
Särkänniemi Adventure Park

On the shores of Näsijärvi, and still within reasonable walking distance from the centre (alternatively, take bus no. 16 year-round, or no. 4 in summer) is the Särkänniemi Adventure Park, which has no fewer than seven separate attractions, four of which are open year-round. (For the rides and Children's Zoo, *see p163.*)

The **Aquarium** features both Finnish and exotic fish, including piranhas, as well as turtles and other reptiles. More than 200 species are represented in all. Perhaps its most unusual feature is the mangrove swamp tank, complete with regular thunderstorms (*open: all year; admission charge*).

The **Planetarium** uses the latest technology to give a spectacular view of the universe (*open: all year; admission charge*).

The **Dolphinarium** is home to five bottlenose dolphins and stages regular performances. It is the world's northernmost dolphinarium, and the first to use a chlorine-free biological system to maintain water quality (*open: summer; admission charge*).

Also at Särkänniemi is the **Näsinneula observation tower**, the highest in the Nordic countries, and something of a symbol of the city. Standing 168m

Tampere

Hämeenlinna Castle

(560ft) tall, it affords a great view of the city and the surrounding lakes and ridges (*open: all year; admission charge*). There is a revolving restaurant, **Ravintola Näsinneula**, which is highly rated for its food.
Contact details for all the above:
Särkänniemi, 33230 Tampere.
Tel: (0) 2 07 130 200;
www.sarkanniemi.fi

The Sara Hildén art museum
The final attraction on the Särkänniemi roster is also the quietest. The Sara Hildén art museum is a collection of Finnish and foreign contemporary art housed in a custom-built centre opened in 1979.
Särkänniemi, 33230 Tampere.
Tel: (0) 3 5654 3500;
www.tampere.fi/hilden/index.html.
Open: Tue–Sun.
Admission charge.

HÄMEENLINNA
Between Tampere and Helsinki is the town of Hämeenlinna, significant as the birthplace of Jean Sibelius and more so for the mighty fortress that gives the town its name. Travellers by train can get a grand view of the castle on their left when coming from Helsinki, and vice versa in the opposite direction.

Birthplace of Jean Sibelius
In the centre of Hämeenlinna is the house in which Jean Sibelius was born. It dates from 1834, but is furnished as it would have been in the 1870s when Sibelius was growing up. It has a collection of documents, photographs and other memorabilia from the composer's early years.
Hallituskatu 11, 13100 Hämeenlinna.
Tel: (0) 3 621 2528;
www.hameenlinna.fi/historiallinenmuseo/
english. Open: daily. Admission charge.

Hämeenlinna fortress

One of the most impressive and ancient fortresses in Finland, Hämeenlinna fortress owes its origins to the great Swedish 'crusades' of the early Middle Ages, as does Turku castle (and Vyborg/Viipuri, now in Russia). The second crusade took place some time in the mid-13th century and it was then that it was decided to establish a castle in the productive Häme province. Initially the castle was part of a defence line, but after the treaty of 1323, when the border with Novgorod was moved further east, it became more of an administrative centre.

Two impressions are paramount as one approaches the castle. First is its great mass and height. The cliché term 'forbidding' seems apt, heightened by the fact that the first buildings one sees were built as prison-houses. Second, the castle is made almost entirely of brick, which sets it apart from the other great fortresses of Finland.

The use of brick is partly due to the local geology, but it also shows a strong German influence; indeed, much of the work was undertaken by German craftsmen.

The construction of the castle took place in several phases: the original fortified camp was augmented in the late 13th century by a series of vaulted brick rooms, including the main hall. Much of this phase of building is intact, making it the best surviving example of medieval life in Finland.

The next phase was the brick castle, which includes some of the most impressive rooms. The unusual style represents a high point in Hämeenlinna's history. From the 17th century onwards, its importance gradually declined. Under Russian rule, the main fort was converted to serve as a prison and later new prison wings were added. Major restoration work was carried out between 1965 and 1979 and brought the castle to its present appearance.

Museum shop and café open: summer. Kustaallin katu 6, 13100 Hämeenlinna. Tel: (0) 3 675 6820; www.nba.fi/en/hame_castle. Open: daily. Admission charge. Guided tours in English usually available.

Buildings around the castle house the region's **Historical Museum**, the **National Prison Museum** and the **Artillery Museum**.

Lake cruises

Hämeenlinna offers several lake cruises. On summer evenings on the relatively small Lake Vanajauesi, there is the chance of a short cruise with great views of the fortress and surrounding scenery (*Merry Lakelines Oy, Passenger harbour, Arvi Karistonkatu 8. Tel: (0) 20 7411 770*).

There is also the possibility of longer cruises on the interconnected lake system to Tampere. These take about eight hours, including an hour's stop at Visavuori (*Finnish Silverline, Laukontori 10 A 3, 33200 Tampere. Tel: (0) 3 212 4804; www.hopealinja.fi/sivut/english/home.htm*).

Southeast Finland and the Lake District

This region encompassing the entire coast east of Helsinki is dotted with harbours great and small, and fringed with archipelagos. Not far inland is a section of the famous King's Road – the king in question being the Swedish monarch, whose rule at its height held sway over territory stretching from the Atlantic coast of Norway to lands that are now part of Russia.

Repovesi National Park

For centuries The King's Road was the principal axis of southern Finland, and in many ways it still is. It was travelled not only by kings and their retinue but by merchants, warriors, pilgrims and poets. The Finnish section of The King's Road crosses the many islands to Turku and then on to Helsinki. Its eastern half takes in Porvoo (*see pp56–9*) and continues through Loviisa, Kotka and Hamina. Like other great 'roads' – most famously the Silk Road of Central Asia – it is in places more a network of parallel routes than a single road. The modern highway that runs east from Helsinki follows the same general direction, but one can get a much better flavour of the historic route by using the minor roads (*see pp108–9*).

Inland, one doesn't have to travel very far before encountering a lake. It is here that the majority of Finland's 180,000 lakes are to be found, including Lake Saimaa, the largest of them all. In fact, Saimaa looks more like a network

Southeast Finland and the Lake District

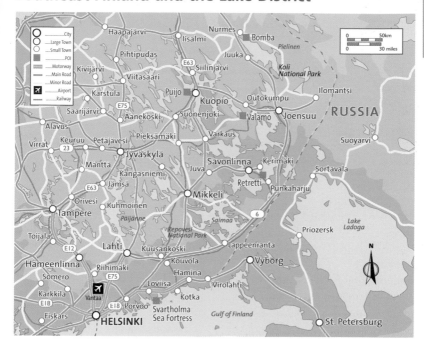

Southeast Finland and the Lake District

of interconnected lakes than a single lake. Islands and peninsulas break up the expanse of this and most other large lakes, so it is difficult to get a clear picture of their true scale, except from above – either from the air or from a high vantage point like Koli Hill or the Puijo Tower in Kuopio.

A slower but more rewarding way to come to grips with this vast, tangled landscape is from the water, and a visit to the Lake District is not complete without at least one journey on the water. It is hard to beat paddling your own canoe, but you can also do it the easy way, aboard one of the many cruise vessels that ply the lakes in summer.

In winter the shallow lakes freeze readily and become travel corridors of a different kind, with an extensive network of routes for skis and snowmobiles.

In the east is Karelia, a region that is strangely both peripheral and central. Most of Karelia lies beyond the border in Russia, and only a small part of it has ever been in Finland. Yet Karelia is crucial to the Finnish national identity. (*For more on its cultural significance see pp126–7.*) For the visitor it is a highly distinctive region, one that is marked by Orthodox churches and monasteries, and also by a richly decorative architectural style.

Tour: Drive or cycle The King's Road

This route is primarily for motorists but can easily be followed by cyclists as well as it mostly uses minor roads. Drivers can make a fast return to Helsinki along the main highway, or head north to Lappeenranta. Cyclists will probably want to finish at Kotka, as there are convenient trains (via Kouvola) back to Helsinki from there.

The King's Road passes through Vantaa, close to Helsinki airport, but the start here is described from Tikkurila, a few kilometres to the east, with frequent trains to/from Helsinki. The distance is about 190km (118 miles); covering it in a day by car is certainly possible, but it is more rewarding to take two or more days. Cyclists should allow for 4–5 days to Kotka.

Follow minor roads towards the east, and after crossing the Helsinki–Tampere motorway, go north a few kilometres on highway 140. Follow road 1321 to Sipoo.

1 Sipoo

Sipoo has two churches, set a few hundred metres apart, amid rolling farmland. The older church, built of stone, is among the oldest medieval churches in Finland. The new, much larger church dates from 1885 and is built of brick.

Follow road 1531 through Anttila and Hinthaara before joining highway 55 for the last few kilometres into Porvoo.

2 Porvoo

The historic Old Town of Porvoo still looks much the same, in many respects, as it would have done to travellers in the heyday of The King's Road. However, the existence of a preserved railway just across the river is ironic, as it was the coming of the railways that marked the beginning of the end of the strategic role of the Road.

Take road 170 through Ilola and Koskenkylä and swing south. Take road 1581 through Pernaja and then rejoin 170 into Loviisa.

3 Loviisa

Look out for the Degerby Manor in the Old Town, part of which is the oldest building in Loviisa. Manors like this often played host to the grander travellers on The King's Road.

Follow the main road east (avoidable for cycles) as far as Pyhtää, then swing south through Länsikylä. Rejoin the main road for a few kilometres and then take 170

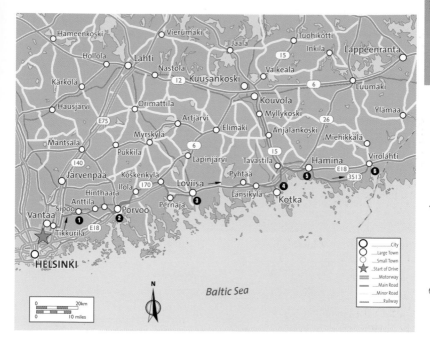

Baltic Sea

○	City
○	Large Town
○	Small Town
★	Start of Drive
▭	Motorway
—	Main Road
⋯	Minor Road
—	Railway

0 ___ 20km
0 ___ 10 miles

N

north of Kotka, with or without a side-trip into Kotka itself.

4 Kotka

The detour into Kotka is highly recommended. For those on bikes it is an easy place from which to return to Helsinki; for all travellers it has a fine harbour and the marvellous Maretarium (*see p112*). It is also possible to take a boat trip out into the Eastern Gulf of Finland National Park.

Continue on road 170, which runs parallel to the new highway and carries light traffic, all the way to Hamina.

5 Hamina

Just 40km (25 miles) from the current Russian border, the town of Hamina

was fortified by the Swedes in the 1720s and the ground plan still remains, the star-like fortifications surrounding a circular town with eight radial streets. *Follow the coast southward and then go east along road 3513 to Virolahti.*

6 Virolahti

Virolahti is the last town before the Russian border. The crossing at Vaalimaa is the busiest on the Russo-Finnish border, with close to 1.5 million people now crossing each year. There has been rapid development, especially of shopping facilities, on the Finnish side.

From here it is possible to return directly to Helsinki on the main highway, or perhaps head north to Lappeenranta.

A quiet street in the Old Town, Loviisa

LOVIISA

Loviisa is a bilingual town (its Swedish name is Lovisa), founded in 1745. Originally called Degerby, it was renamed by King Adolf Fredrik of Sweden after his queen. The town was familiar to Jean Sibelius, who spent many summer holidays here in his youth, and composed the *Kullervo Symphony* here. It is no surprise, then, that it hosts a Sibelius Festival every year in June, with a focus on chamber music rather than the more famous orchestral works.

Loviisa is one of those places that springs to life in the summer, and by the end of August it starts to get pretty somnolent. The streets are lined with venerable wooden houses, but the historic heart of the Old Town is between the Laivasilta area and the modern centre. It is all contained within ten minutes' walking distance.

Laivasilta

The area called Laivasilta, a few minutes' walk from the town centre, was the centre of the town's maritime trade from 1745 onwards. The harbour is now a lively yachting marina during the summer months.

A number of the original warehouses have been rebuilt and house summer galleries, cafés, restaurants and the small but pleasant **Maritime Museum**, which documents the town's seafaring history (*tel: (0) 19 533 188; www. loviisa.fi; open: Fri and weekends in summer and by special arrangement for groups; admission charge*).

The Loviisa Town Museum

The museum has sections relating to the founding of the town, the Svartholma fortress, and tin and silver production in Loviisa. Local Gustavian furniture and items from the spa period are also on display. The museum also has a small exhibition about the young Jean Sibelius.

Puistokatu 2. Tel: (0) 19 555 357; www.loviisa.fi. Open: summer Tue–Sun, winter Sun except during special exhibitions. Admission charge.

Sibelius House

The house where Sibelius spent his summer holidays and wrote *Kullervo* – now called Sibelius House – stands by a traffic intersection; no doubt it was more peaceful in his day.

Sibeliusenkatu 10.
Tel: (0) 19 555 499.
Open: summer. Admission charge.

Svartholma sea fortress

Loviisa's main attraction is the Svartholma sea fortress. Construction began in 1748 according to plans drawn up by Augustin Ehrensvärd, also the architect of Suomenlinna in Helsinki,

so it is no surprise that Svartholma is a bit of a mini-Suomenlinna.

Cynics might wonder if there is a fundamental flaw in Ehrensvärd's designs because, like Suomenlinna, Svartholma surrendered to the Russians with barely a shot being fired. For a period the fortress was used as a prison and a garrison before being abandoned in 1855. During the Crimean War it was blown up by the British and fell into decay, but has now been extensively restored.

The only way to visit Svartholma is by boat: trips run from Laivasilta marina several times a day in June, July and August, and there is a special 'children's cruise' in the mornings. The journey takes about 45 minutes.

Because the fortress is largely undisturbed for most of the year, it has become a place of considerable botanical interest (*special tours*

The jetty in Loviisa

available, normally only in Finnish and Swedish). There is an exhibition about the history of the fortress. There is also a small shop and restaurant. *Tel: (0) 40 532 1135; www.svartholm.fi. Free admission. Guided tours are available for a charge.*

KOTKA

Kotka shelters behind a charming archipelago, part of which is a national park of great importance for both nesting and migratory birds. It is a port well used by commercial traffic, as well as a focus for yachting in the eastern Gulf of Finland. It hosts a noted maritime festival at the end of July. Sea cruises and fishing trips are popular. If sea shanties are your thing, you will not want to miss one of the sing-along cruises. The town centre is compact and pleasant, but it is the small-boat harbour that is the main draw. This is attractively laid out and presents a lively scene for a longer season than many of its counterparts.

Kantasatama Quay

A short walk north, across the town centre, is the Kantasatama Quay. From 2008, the area will be home to a new museum centre incorporating the Kotka Provincial Museum and the National Maritime Museum.

Here also is the the world's oldest surviving icebreaker, *Tarmo*. This steam-powered vessel was built at Newcastle upon Tyne in 1907 and served for many decades, including both world wars. She was turned into a museum but recalled to active duty during the exceptionally severe winter of 1970.
Tel: (0) 5 234 4405. Open: summer. Admission charge.

Kotka Maretarium

Apart from being a starting point for a tour of the idyllic archipelago, Kotka is home to the Kotka Maretarium. Opened in 2002, the striking building stands right by the harbour. It is reckoned to be Finland's finest aquarium, and is an excellent place to learn about the marine life of the surrounding waters.

A highlight is the massive Baltic Tank, 7m (23ft) deep and containing half a million litres (110,000 gallons) of water. The Maretarium also has a marine theatre, exhibits on fish research, an aquatic souvenir store, Café Ariela, and

Kotka Maretarium

a research and nature study centre.
Sapokankatu 2, 48100 Kotka.
Tel: (0) 40 311 0330;
www.maretarium.fi.
*Open: all year. Admission charge. Guided
tours available in English, can be pre-
booked by phone or website.*

THE LAKE DISTRICT

Finland's Lake District certainly knocks
the spots off its English namesake in
numerical terms. Although precise
numbers depend on where you draw
the boundaries, and lakes are hardly
scarce elsewhere in southern Finland,
there are many thousands of greater
and lesser lakes in this region.

The big daddy is Lake Saimaa,
Finland's largest by a considerable
margin. From a casual glance at the
map it may be far from obvious that it
is a single lake, appearing more like a
maze of smaller lakes and channels, but
since none of those channels represents
a change in water level, it is all one.
Adding to its complexity is the number
of islands – 13,710 of them. Some are
mere skerries, but others have
substantial populations: between them
they are home to around 20,000 people.
There are more islands, covering a
greater surface area, in Lake Saimaa
than there are in the Åland archipelago.

Including the islands, Lake Saimaa
has a shoreline of 14,850km (9,227
miles). For all its spread, however,
it is shallow, with an average depth
of just 12m (39ft) and a maximum
of 85m (279ft).

The coastline near Kotka

Lappeenranta

Arrive at Lappeenranta by car and you
might be forgiven for thinking you've
stumbled into a concrete jungle, made
up entirely of intersections and
underpasses. But first impressions are
misleading, and on foot it is a
considerably more amiable place, with
much to admire and enjoy. It is
particularly known for the many linden
trees (lime trees in British parlance)
that line the streets.

Lappeenranta is the centre of
south Karelia, a thriving region that
trades heavily on its proximity to

A DAY IN RUSSIA

While the lake cruises from Lappeenranta are
pretty standard fare, albeit with some
gorgeous scenery, a cruise through the Saimaa
Canal is different. It takes you into Russia,
with the chance to spend a few hours in the
fascinating Old Town of Vyborg (known as
Viipuri when it was in Finnish hands).
Cruises run from approximately 20 May to
10 September. All visitors to Russia need a
visa, but for citizens of EU countries these can
be arranged by the cruise operator – all they
need is a copy of your passport a few days
in advance.

Part of the fortress area at Lappeenranta

St Petersburg. Standing on the southern shore of Lake Saimaa and at the terminus of the Saimaa Canal, Lappeenranta is a hub for commercial traffic as well as for a variety of pleasure cruises: the most unusual are those that travel along the Saimaa Canal into Russia.

The **Saimaa Canal**, which links Finland's lake system to the Baltic, is 43km (26^1/$_2$ miles) long, with half of that in Russia, and has eight locks.

The town was established at the site of an existing trading post in 1649 by Count Per Brahe (a prolific 'establisher', so to speak) but it soon lost out to its rival Vyborg (Viipuri) and became subsumed under Russia proper, rather than being part of the autonomous Grand Duchy of Finland. It returned to Finnish hands only in 1917.

Linnoitus

The big attraction of Lappeenranta is its fortress (Linnoitus). While the name might lead you to expect a castle, what you will find is more of a fortified town, or at least an elevated neighbourhood, surrounded by massive bastions. It doesn't make for an impression of monumentality in the way that Savonlinna, further up Lake Saimaa, does. Interest lies more in the individual buildings and in what they contain. In summer, it presents a lively scene and you may well see cavalrymen riding through in elaborately embroidered jackets. In winter it is a lot quieter, but the area is always open to visitors.

The site includes cafés, workshops and several museums. The **Cavalry Museum** is housed in the town's oldest building, dating from 1772, and was originally a guardhouse.

Kristiinankatu 2, 53100 Lappeenranta. Tel: (0) 5616 2257; www.ekarjala.fi/museot/eng/lappeenranta/ratsuvakimuseo.html. Open: daily summer, winter by prior arrangement. Admission charge.

Orthodox church

Pride of place, at least in terms of intrinsic beauty, surely goes to the tiny, almost doll-like, Orthodox church. This is the oldest Orthodox church in Finland (1785) and, externally at least, one of the plainest – it was built by the members of the garrison themselves.

A group of buildings below the northern gate of the church houses craft workshops, cafés and so on. There is no need to walk back up to the fortress from the church: instead, you can stroll round to the quay, directly below the eastern side of the fortress, from where the various cruise ships operate. Next to this is a seasonal marketplace and, moving further round the shoreline, a small-boat marina.

Saimaa Canal Museum

If you are planning a trip through the Saimaa Canal to Russia, it is worth taking a look at the Saimaa Canal Museum.
Sulkuvartijankatu 16, 53300 Lappeenranta. Tel: (0) 204 48 3115; www.ekarjala.fi/museot/eng. Open: daily summer. Admission charge.

South Carelian Museum

The South Carelian Museum (the spelling of Karelia varies) includes collections focusing not only on Lappeenranta, but also on Viipuri (Vyborg), now in Russia. There is a huge, fascinating scale model of Vyborg, a snapshot of the town as it stood at midday on 2 September 1939.

Kristiinankatu 15, 53101 Lappeenranta. Tel: (0) 5616 2255; www.ekarjala.fi/museot/eng. Open: daily summer, Tue–Sun rest of the year.

South Karelian Art Museum

The South Karelian Art Museum is housed in a barracks building of 1798, and has an extensive collection of both traditional and modern art.
Kristiinankatu 8–10, 53101 Lappeenranta. Tel: (0) 5616 2256; www.ekarjala.fi/museot/eng. Open: daily summer, Tue–Sun rest of the year. Admission charge, free for children under 16.

Kuutinkanava in Repovesi National Park

Repovesi National Park

The Repovesi National Park (Repoveden kansallispuisto) lies roughly midway between Kotka and Mikkeli, with the nearest sizeable town being Kouvola. It is an area of almost 30sq km (11¹/₂sq miles), known as the largest undisturbed area of crag, lake, forest and bog in the south of the country. It is a haunt for beavers and flying squirrels, foxes and eagles, but for the average visitor it is the wonderful scenery that is most likely to make an impression.

While we have described a walk here (*see pp124–5*), it is possibly even better suited to exploring by boat.

Mikkeli

There are two reasons to visit Mikkeli. If you are interested in Finnish history then it is not to be missed, as it was the headquarters of the Finnish army during World War II. It is also a good place to start a trip into the wilds of the lake region, whether for fishing, canoeing or just trekking.

Jalkaväkimuseo

The Infantry Museum (Jalkaväkimuseo) is a general military museum. If you are interested in uniforms, guns and similar military exhibits, you will love it; otherwise it is of limited interest.
Jääkärinkatu 6–8, 50100 Mikkeli. Tel: (0) 15 369 666; www.jalkavakimuseo.fi. Open: Fri–Sun; mid-May–end Aug daily. Admission charge, free for children under 7.

Päämajamuseo

Mikkeli's pivotal role in the war is commemorated by two museums, of

Headquarters of the Finnish Army in World War II

which the more specifically relevant is the Headquarters Museum (Päämajamuseo), suitably housed in the very building (the Central Elementary School) from which the legendary General Mannerheim oversaw the Winter War. Extensive use of film and sound archives and modern multimedia ensures that the museum is far from static.

Päämajankuja 1–3, 50100 Mikkeli. Tel: (0) 15 194 2427; www.mikkeli.fi/fi/museot/english/02_the_headquarters_museum. Open: summer daily, rest of the year Fri–Sun. Admission charge, children free.

Punkaharju Ridge

When you travel from Lappeenranta to Savonlinna, whether by road or by rail, you can't fail to notice the Punkaharju Ridge. The words 'Ice Age' are usually inserted before 'Ridge', pointing to its origins, but then the same can be said of nearly every prominent feature of the Finnish landscape. The narrow, sinuous ridge, about 7km (4¹/₄ miles) in length, is a good example of an esker – a ridge of sand or gravel left by a river flowing under an ice sheet. There are hundreds of eskers in Finland: one is displayed in the famous view from Koli Hill (*see p122*). The significance of Punkaharju lies in its role as a natural causeway, which has given it great strategic importance in this region of fluctuating borders. To travel the full length of the ridge, take the minor road that leaves the main highway just north

of Punkaharju village, as north of the halfway point the highway and railway diverge onto an artificial causeway. *There is a visitors' centre at the old railway station near the north end of the ridge.*

Lusto

Close by is Lusto, the Finnish Forest Museum. There is a railway halt here. Its permanent display is complemented by a changing programme of special exhibitions. There are some pleasant and short walking trails in the area, and the centre hires out boats and bikes, which are ideal for exploring the surrounding landscape. There is also a museum shop and restaurant.

58450 Punkaharju. Tel: (0) 15 345 000; www.lusto.fi. Open: Feb–Dec. Admission charge.

Retretti

An easy walk away is one of Finland's, if not the world's, most unusual art galleries, Retretti, housed in a huge artificial cave. It is open only in the summer, and the exhibition, which changes every year, is usually of international standard. Even if you are here out of season it is worth taking a detour up the Retretti road to see the huge sculptured figures created from what appear to be natural boulders. Retretti has its own railway halt just 300m (330yds) away, and there is a bus stop about 500m (550yds) away. You can also get there on a steamboat from Savonlinna.

58450 Punkaharju.
Tel: (0) 15 77522 00. www.retretti.fi.
Open: June–Aug daily. Admission charge.

Savonlinna

Savonlinna has two outstanding claims to fame. One is Olavinlinna Castle, said to be the finest castle in Finland. The other is its Opera Festival, which more or less takes over the whole town for a full month in summer (early July–early August). For more details *see* Festivals, *pp24–5.* As you might expect, accommodation is scarce and expensive during the Festival, and if you are visiting for other reasons it may be better to avoid this period, or maybe nip in and out by train for the day.

Dollmuseum Suruton

Among Savonlinna's other attractions is the Dollmuseum Suruton, housed in a century-old wooden villa, and home to over 1,000 dolls and a similar number of other toys.
Kylpylaitoksentie 2, 57130 Savonlinna.
Tel: (0) 15 273 960;
www.savonlinna.fi/kulttuuripalvelut/
suruton.htm.
Open: summer daily. Admission charge.

Nestori (Saimaa Nature Centre)

Just 50m (55yds) or so from the castle is Nestori, the Saimaa Nature Centre. Housed in a pleasing old villa, this has a small but information-packed display of the natural history of the Saimaa region, with special emphasis on its rarest denizen, the Saimaa ringed seal. Ringed

Olavinlinna fortress

seals are the most numerous seal species in the world but the Saimaa subspecies, which has evolved in isolation for millennia, is extremely scarce. There are only around 270 at present, but these numbers have recovered from a minimum of below 200, and there is good reason to hope that they will continue to do so. The Saimaa ringed seal population is concentrated in the Savonlinna region. They hunt through the winter in the water below the ice and give birth in midwinter.

There is usually a temporary art exhibition on the upper floor at Nestori. There is also a small shop, and in summer several cafés are open close by. A variety of lake cruises departs during the summer season from a wharf about five minutes' walk away.
Aino Ackten puistotie 4, 57130
Savonlinna. Tel: (0) 205 645 929.
Open: all year, except Mon out of season.
Free admission.

Olavinlinna

Olavinlinna – the fortress of St Olaf – stands massively on an island athwart a narrow channel connecting two of the major basins of Lake Saimaa. This was a vital strategic position even before the castle was completed in 1475, and the waterway remains in use today, by commercial craft and pleasure cruisers.

Olavinlinna was founded by the Dane Erik Axelsson Toft, Governor of Vyborg. Before building of the stone castle was begun, a wooden fortification was erected to protect the builders from Russian attacks. It saw action repeatedly through the following centuries, holding out until 1714, when it surrendered after a protracted siege. Subsequently it changed hands several times under successive treaties. Its military importance declined after 1809 when Finland fell under Russian dominion. Subsequent neglect led to a growing need for restoration, which was undertaken on a large scale in the 1960s and 70s. It first hosted opera performances in 1912.

A famous legend attaches to Olavinlinna, about a young girl who was walled alive as punishment for treason. A rowan tree sprang up from the spot where she was immured, its white flowers said to symbolise her innocence, its red berries her blood. Sadly, the tree no longer survives.

There are two small museums within the castle, one devoted to the fortress itself, the other to the Orthodox church. In summer, a gift shop opens. After the castle closes for the evening, the pontoon is swung aside and it is worth wandering along the facing shore to get a better impression of its imposing isolation. *FI-57150 Olavinlinna. Tel: (0) 15 531 164; www.nba.fi/en/olavinlinna_castle. Open: daily. Admission charge, free on 18 May (International Museum Day) and 29 July (St Olaf's Day). Guided tours in English available in the summer.*

Kerimäki

Twenty kilometres (12½ miles) from Savonlinna is the village of Kerimäki, noted for being the site of the world's largest wooden church. Cynics might describe it as one of the world's largest white elephants. It appears to be the result of colossal hubris on the part of its builders, who confidently assumed that virtually the entire population of the far-flung parish would assemble there regularly. The miscalculation quickly became obvious, and a much smaller church was tacked on behind. The main church is impossible to heat and is used

The colossal wooden church at Kerimäki

only in summer. It has hardly ever been filled to capacity: it has seats for 3,000; with standees, it can accommodate 5,000 people (*58200 Kerimäki; tel: (0)15 578 9111; open: summer daily*).

Kuopio

Kuopio is a major regional centre, lying at the northern end of the Lake Saimaa waterway system – which, the locals will tell you, is the more scenic end. One of the most appropriate, most leisurely and nicest ways to arrive (or leave) is by boat. In summer there are regular cruises to and from Savonlinna. This is a full-day trip (10½ hours) and the longest regular passenger route on Finnish inland waterways. If you don't have that much time, there is a wide range of other lake cruises to choose from – around 20 different options at the last count, all based at the passenger harbour. The harbour area is also a pleasant place for strolling. In summer there is lots of bustle, but once August has passed it reverts to being much more peaceful.

Kuopio Museum

Kuopio Museum is two museums in one: the Museum of Cultural History and the Museum of Natural History share this very attractive art nouveau building. There is more than a hint of a castle about the building, designed by J V Stromberg and completed in 1907. *Kauppakatu 23, 70100 Kuopio. Tel: (0) 17 152 603; http://kuopionmuseo.fi. Open: daily; winter Sun–Fri. Admission charge.*

Orthodox Church Museum

The Orthodox Church Museum of Finland is the largest such museum in the western world, testament to the importance of the Eastern Church in Karelia. The collection derives principally from objects in possession of the Monastery of Valamo, and consist largely of 18th- and 19th-century material. There is a huge collection of icons, gold and silver objects, and lavishly decorated vestments, altar cloths and other textiles. *Karjalankatu 1, 70110 Kuopio. Tel: (0) 17 287 2244; www.ort.fi/kirkkomuseo. Guided tours available by arrangement. Open: daily summer, rest of the year Tue–Sun. Admission charge.*

Puijo Tower

Kuopio's great landmark is the Puijo Tower, standing prominently atop the hill of the same name. At 306m (1,004ft) above sea level, it is one of the highest points in southern Finland, and for an unobstructed 360° panoramic view it has no real rival. The present tower is the third to stand on this spot. The first, built in 1856, was of wood and a modest 16m (52ft) high. It was replaced by a 24m (79ft) stone tower in 1906. The present tower, all 75m (246ft) of it, was completed in 1963.

There is an open viewing platform at the top, a café on the floor below, and a decent à la carte restaurant below that. *Tel: (0) 17 255 5250. Open: daily. Admission charge.*

The harbour at Kuopio, looking towards Puijo Tower

From the viewing deck you can get a bird's-eye view of the nearby ski jumps. Every major ski resort has these, but the ones at Kuopio are among the most accessible. There is action here even when there is no snow as the jumpers train even in summer, with the snow replaced by special matting. You can walk down the hill to the base of the jumps for a better view and then take the chairlift back up.

There are several lakes, rivers and rapids within easy reach of Kuopio, making it a good base if you would like to do some fishing.

Monastery of Valamo

The Monastery of Valamo, in the district of Heinävesi, is the only Orthodox monastery in Finland. Its origins can be traced to a monastery founded on an island in Lake Ladoga, in Russian Karelia. Its exact age is uncertain, but it is probably over 800 years old. The unfriendly attitude of the Soviet state led to the community being evacuated to Finland during the war in 1940. Russian was then the dominant language, but since the 1970s the monastery has adopted Finnish for worship and general communication.

The monastery has a café-restaurant and souvenir shop. It also has its own hotel and guesthouse.
Valamontie 42, 79850 Uusi-Valamo.
Tel: (0) 17 570 1810; www.valamo.fi.
Open: daily. Admission free. Guided tours in English can be arranged.

Joensuu

Joensuu is the capital of north Karelia province, and an essential port of call for anyone seeking to understand the background to this region, marked by fluctuating borders and shifting allegiances (*see pp126–7*).

North Karelia Museum

The interior of the North Karelia Museum or Carelicum belies its drab and functional exterior: inside there is an impressive atrium, and on the second floor is arranged a well-judged series of displays. The principal section is titled 'Karelia: Both Sides of the Border', reflecting the fact that much of Karelia is today in Russia. The story of the region is told through a mix of modern media, coupled with historic artefacts ranging from the Iron Age to the conflicts of 1939–45. Striking evidence of the great privation endured by millions of Finns during the Winter War and Continuation War is provided by the exhibits of clothes made of paper and wood-soled shoes.

The other part of the exhibition is called 'Karelia – Land of Inspiration', and it explores the pivotal influence of the Karelian landscape and culture on various composers, writers and artists, from the *Kalevala* compiler Elias Lönnrot to Jean Sibelius and beyond. There is a nice café in the atrium and a small shop.

Koskikatu 5, 80100 Joensuu.
Tel: (0) 13 267 5222; www.carelicum.fi.
Open: daily. Admission charge.

Koli National Park

No place exemplifies the significance of the Karelian landscape better than Koli National Park and, above all, the hill, Ukko-Koli, which lies at its centre. At 347m (1,138ft), it is the highest point in southern Finland, and commands extensive views over the surrounding terrain. Craggy outcrops of white quartzite provide great vantage points. The area is a tapestry of many different habitats with a long tradition of slash-and-burn cultivation, and supports an unusually wide variety of birds.

The area became a tourist attraction during the late 19th century, and its place in the Finnish soul was firmly established when Sibelius came here on his honeymoon.

There is easy access to the upper reaches of Ukko-Koli. From large car parks halfway up the hill, a striking aerial tramway (*free*) climbs the short distance to the ridge. You can also walk up; it is not far.

There is a hotel at the top, and also the Heritage Centre (*see below*). Marked trails lead the short distance to the main summit, but often it is just a case of following the crowds. To appreciate the scenery in peace it's advisable to follow one of the longer walking trails, marked on a large map beside the hotel.

The summit ridge can also be reached from the shores of Lake Pielinen by using the chairlift, which operates in summer, of the Koli ski area (which has a handful of short but steep runs).

Coaches from Joensuu and Kajaani run regular services to the area; there is also a dedicated and inexpensive minibus service (*tel: (0) 100 9986*). The most romantic way to arrive is by boat; in summer, there are services from Joensuu, Lieksa, Nurmes and Vuonislahti (*www.saimaaferries.fi*).

Heritage Centre Ukko

Heritage Centre Ukko, occupying a striking modern building, dispenses information on the local landscape as well as surrounding areas in eastern Finland. There is a nice little café and a

souvenir shop with a strong emphasis on high-quality, ecofriendly handicrafts.
Ylä-Kolintie 39, 83960 Koli.
Tel: (0) 10 211 3200; www.koli.fi/en.
Open: daily. Admission charge for main exhibition.

Ilomantsi

The little town of Ilomantsi is the most easterly in Finland. Not surprisingly, the Karelian and Orthodox traditions are at their strongest here. It lies in a lovely region that typifies the Karelian scenery, and is a good base for hikes and treks into the wilderness.

The town itself was almost completely destroyed during World War II. It was rebuilt without much style, but on a hill just outside the town is the re-created Karelian village of Parppeinvaara.

Parppeinvaara

This is an assemblage of traditional buildings, peopled by characters in Karelian costume. Buildings include the Rune-singer's House and an Orthodox prayer hut (*tsasouna*). There is an exhibition illustrating the tales of the *Kalevala*, for which there could not be a more appropriate setting. Performances on the stringed kantele and folk-singing take place regularly. There is a handicraft shop on site and a restaurant which serves Karelian specialities nearby.
Parppeintie 1, 82900 Ilomantsi.
Tel: (0) 400 240 072.
Open: daily summer, rest of the year by arrangement. Admission charge.

Sibelius Hall

Lahti

Lahti is a bustling city, and a major winter sports centre. It is also one of the nearest bases to Helsinki from where lake cruises operate (e.g. to Jyväskylä).

Its main claim to fame is that it is the home of one of Finland's leading orchestras, appropriately based in the striking Sibelius Hall.

Sibelius Hall

This is a must-see for anyone interested in architecture as it represents a striking fusion of old and new. Alongside the restored century-old woodworking factory is the striking new building. Its exterior is almost entirely of glass, allowing a clear view of the tremendous wooden structure that supports it. There is a gift shop and café.
Ankkurikatu 7, 15140 Lahti.
Tel: (0)3 814 2801; www.sibeliustalo.fi.
Open: daily.

Walk: Repovesi National Park

This walk measures only about 8km (5 miles) on the map, but it offers a great mix of fine forest, glittering lakes, secluded tarns and spectacular crags. There are some steep gradients and a lot of the going is pretty rough, so sturdy footwear is recommended.

Time: 3 hours.

Getting there is easy if you have your own transport. The start at Lapinsalmi, is well signposted off the 368 road.

For those without a car, there are buses from Kouvola. Rather than walking down the spur road described above, it is better to aim for the former railway halt 5km (3 miles) north at Hillosensalmi, where there is also an information point. There is a walking trail from here to Lapinsalmi but this doubles the length of the walk. A better bet in summer is the waterbus service (May–Sept). This will drop you at Lapinsalmi (point 1). You can also arrange for a water-taxi (*tel: (0) 400 551 530*).

Walk through the 'gateway' and after less than 100m (110yds) take the left fork, up the steps and along duckboards, and continue above the water to a suspension bridge. Cross this and descend right to a clearing.

1 Lapinsalmi

The clearing has a shelter and fireplace, landing stages and, set back in the forest, a long-drop toilet. It is also a stop on the waterbus route. A beautiful spot, but often busy.

Follow the sign for WC and then pick up a track used by park vehicles. Follow this until it leads to a broader forest road. Just to the left is the small lake of Katajajärvi. After about 1km (²/₃ mile) the road passes between another tarn on the left and a swamp on the right. Not too far beyond this is a flight of steps that climbs up to the left.

2 Forest path

The steps lead to the finest forest walking on the route, with open stands of Scots Pine on the rises alternating with sheltered, damper hollows where broad-leaved trees such as aspen and lime can be found.

Follow the path from the steps, twisting and turning but always well marked with blue tape or paint, until it finally drops down to another forest road.

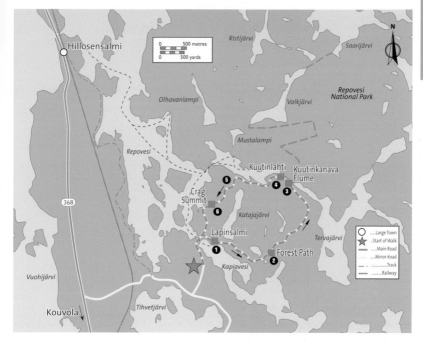

3 Kuutinkanava flume

In bygone times, floating the logs was the easiest way to transport the timber. A number of flumes were built to avoid logs snagging on the rocky rapids between lakes. The Kuutinkanava flume is one of the best surviving examples, linking Tervajärvi, just to the right as you arrive, with Repovesi.

Follow a broad path beside the flume, soon leading to shelters and landing stages at Kuutinlahti.

4 Kuutinlahti

Kuutinlahti is an arm of the Repovesi lake. The view across the water is dominated by a steep crag, and a litter of huge granite blocks prised from the precipice by the action of ice.

Bear left along the shoreline. The path negotiates duckboards (some quite rickety) and a broad shelf below a steep lichenous crag. Eventually the path bears away from the water, and forks.

5 Path junction

Both ways have signs for Lapinsalmi but be sure to fork right. Climb again, pass a small tarn with waterlilies and come out suddenly at the top of a steep crag.

6 Crag summit

The crag commands a magnificent view, all the more impressive after the enclosed forests.

Descend the steep wooden stairs to the right of the crag to get back to the suspension bridge.

Karelia

The atrium at the Carelicum Museum in Joensuu

What is Karelia? This is an important question, as 'Karelianism' was one of the major themes of the National Romantic Movement of the 19th century, which largely defined the Finnish national identity and paved the way for independence. Its importance is matched by complexity, as illustrated by a series of old maps reproduced in the Carelicum in Joensuu, all of which show 'Karelia' in different locations. (And, incidentally, by a variety of different spellings.)

It is also worth reflecting on the fact that Finland's eastern border has been redrawn by no fewer than nine different treaties since 1323. At no time has all of Karelia been in Finland, but at times more or less all of it has been in Russia. An odd state of affairs for what seems to be such an essentially Finnish region!

Like Finland itself, one possible way of defining Karelia is through language. There is a recognised Karelian tongue, which is closely related to Finnish – and, therefore, very unlike Russian. However, the ambiguity does not end there, as in parts of Karelia the language traditionally spoken is considered to be a dialect of Finnish.

One can at least say that the Karelians were and are, culturally and linguistically, closely related to the Finns. Over much of the region the dominant population for many centuries has been Karelian, but in some parts there is an extensive Russian presence. Separate Russian and Karelian villages in the same areas were not uncommon.

It appears that Christianity first reached the region in the 11th century, at the time of the great schism between the Catholic and Orthodox churches. While most of Finland fell under Catholic influence (and later became Lutheran), Karelia became, and remained, Orthodox. Ironically, again, during many subsequent conflicts its population supported the Russian rather than the Swedish side, mostly on grounds of common faith – something that changed radically during the Soviet era.

While the risk of oversimplification remains, it is common and helpful to identify three principal divisions. The easiest to pin down is Finnish Karelia, i.e. the part that lies within present-day Finland: essentially the two modern provinces of north and south Karelia, with their capitals at Joensuu and Lappeenranta, respectively. By far the largest segment is Russian Karelia, which historically has nearly always been under Russian control (and that of the preceding Kingdom of Novgorod).

The most sensitive area, at least from the Finnish point of view, is that called 'ceded Karelia'. Even here definitions may vary but the simplest may be to call it the territory that formed part of Finland from 1920 (the Treaty of Turku) until the 1939–45 conflict, and which was yielded under the post-war settlement. This represented a tenth of the land area of Finland; about 400,000 people were displaced when this happened.

One reason for the importance of Karelia to Finnish culture was the survival of the oral tradition, from which Elias Lönnrot compiled the *Kalevala*. The landscapes of the region also inspired many Finnish artists, notably the painter Akseli Gallen-Kallela and the composer Sibelius.

Typical Karelian architecture

Jyväskylä

Jyväskylä is a significant regional centre and a fine base for lake cruises and other outdoor activities. It was also the home and early base of the architect Alvar Aalto. It has more than three dozen of the great man's buildings; it also has a museum dedicated to his life and work.

Having said that, first impressions on arrival can be less than inspiring. Jyväskylä has many drab buildings by lesser architects, and a lot of them seem to be crammed together in one of Finland's more claustrophobic town centres. There is a hint of Soviet functionalism about it, which is at odds with Aalto's humanistic philosophy. It should also be said, however, that it is one of the country's best shopping cities, with everything within easy walking distance.

Architecture buffs may well want to make a swift escape from the centre, and this is best done by walking southwest on Kavelykatu, the pedestrianised street at the heart of the shopping district. This continues to Kauppakatu and then Seminaarinkatu. Here the first university buildings appear on the right, and, in pointed

University buildings in Jyväskylä

Winter beside the lake, Jyväskylä

contrast, pleasant old wooden houses line the left side of the street.

Continue down the street, angling slightly left as it dips under an elevated highway, and immediately after this are two notable Aalto buildings.

Museum of Central Finland (Keski-Suomen Museo)

This is the first one, dating from 1961. Its interest is not solely confined to architecture, as it is full of information about the region and the city.
Alvar Aallon katu 7.
Tel: (0) 14 624 930;
www.jyvaskyla.fi/ksmuseo. Open:
Tue–Sun. Admission charge, free Fri.

Alvar Aalto Museum

Right next door is the Alvar Aalto Museum. Externally it is surprisingly unassertive, though perhaps intentionally, as it focuses on interior design, furniture and other smaller-scale work. It was a central tenet of Aalto's philosophy that all these aspects should be fully integrated.

There is a museum shop which sells a number of Aalto-designed items.
Alvar Aallon katu 7.
Tel: (0) 14 624 809;
www.alvaraalto.fi/index.htm.
Open: Tue–Sun. Admission charge.

Ylistönrinne

Continue down the street opposite the Aalto museum and then turn right along a foot-and-cycle path. Follow this round to the left and soon you will find yourself crossing a bridge (Ylistönsilta). Ahead is another sector of the university, called Ylistönrinne, which includes the departments of physics and chemistry. The white buildings, beautifully arranged along the contours of the hillside, represent a fine development of Aalto's philosophy by later architects.

Passenger Harbour
Another foot-and-cycle path leads in front of the Hotel Alba and then along the shoreline back to the city centre, via the Passenger Harbour. This is where all the summer cruises leave from. Besides out-and-back tours, there are regular services to Lahti, Jämsä, Suolahti and Viitasaari. Cross a glassed-in bridge over road and railway back to the city centre.

Craft Museum of Finland and National Costume Centre
Of the other museums in Jyväskylä, the one most likely to be of interest is the Craft Museum of Finland and National Costume Centre, a comprehensive and self-explanatory title. The permanent craft exhibition here explores the earliest use of tools right through to modern design.
Kauppakatu 25. Tel: (0) 14 624 945; www.craftmuseum.fi. Open: Tue–Sun. Admission charge, free Fri.

Natural History Museum of Central Finland
The Natural History Museum of Central Finland is housed at the base of a water tower atop the hill overlooking the town centre.

Ihantolantie 5. Tel: (0) 14 260 3810; www.jyu.fi/erillis/museo/en/natural. Open: Tue–Sun. Admission charge, free Fri.

Laajavuori
In the outskirts of Jyväskylä is Laajavuori, a small but pleasant ski area. While no one would suggest making it the main reason for a trip to Finland, or even Jyväskylä, if you are in the area in winter it is certainly worth spending a day on its half-dozen runs. It is also the centre of a good network of cross-country trails and is home to one of Finland's most famous ski jumps. It is certainly worth a visit if there is a competition scheduled, but even watching the jumpers in training is impressive.

In summer it offers the unusual experience of Downhill Rally Driving, really a cross between go-karting and bobsleigh. Having ridden up on the ski lift, participants come down the serpentine track in cars powered only by gravity. But, unlike skis, they do have brakes!
Laajavuorentie 15. Tel: (0) 14 624 885; www.laajavuori.com

Old Church at Petäjävesi
The Old Church at Petäjävesi, about 35km (21$^1/_2$ miles) west of Jyväskylä, is one of Finland's five UNESCO World Heritage Sites. A nearby main road does detract a little from what should be a peaceful atmosphere, but this is a minor drawback. It is open only in

summer or by special arrangement, but you can admire its lovely exterior at any time.

Dedicated locals pressed ahead with construction of the church even though they had not received confirmation of funding from Stockholm. Subsequently they raised a national subscription to pay for the completion of the work (including minor niceties like windows!). The church was finished in 1765 and recognised by UNESCO in 1994 as an outstanding example of wooden-church building.

Kirkkotie 12. Tel: (0) 40 582 2461; www.petajavesi.fi/kirkko/en/index.shtml. Open: daily in summer, otherwise by appointment.

A World Heritage Site – the Old Church, Petäjävesi

Into the Arctic

The north of Finland is a thinly populated region. Summer here is a time of 'white nights', when the sun never sets. Winters are long and deep, but it is a mistake to imagine them as a time of perpetual darkness: even at midwinter, the 'daytime' is marked by twilight, and with the snow reflecting the light, it is surprisingly easy to see your way around. Of course it is much easier when there is a moon, and sometimes the nights are brightened by the unearthly beauty of the Northern Lights. But if you really can't do without the sun, make the trip in March, when the snow is still deep but there is plenty of daylight.

There are virtually endless opportunities throughout the region for hiking, biking, rafting, canoeing and fishing. In winter activities include skiing (downhill and cross-country), snowmobiling and whisking along in sleds pulled by eager husky dogs or even by reindeer! Nor should one forget that autumn (*ruska*), with its vivid colours, is one of the most popular times for hiking. The further north one goes, the lower is the tree line and the more open the landscape: for anyone who feels hemmed in by the seemingly endless forests further south, this land of vast spaces and wide horizons is an antidote. The less strenuously inclined can explore the distinctive *Sámi* (Lapp) culture.

Oulu

Oulu is either a gateway *to* the north, or the major centre *in* the north,

according to who you believe. It is certainly the largest city in the northern half of the country, and it is the capital of a large province which stretches right across to the Russian frontier, and includes some fine scenery. However, the city itself is neither Lappish nor Arctic, and struggles to a claim for attention, except as a staging post. It has good train connections from Helsinki, including sleeper services, and good onward bus connections to destinations like Kuusamo and Ruka.

Kemi

About 100km (62 miles) further north, and on the same rail line, Kemi has a unique claim to fame, as the home port of the icebreaker *Sampo*, the only one in the world that doubles as a cruise vessel. Regular trips lasting about four hours are offered from mid-December

to the end of April. The high points include a walk on the ice and, for the brave, a dip in the icy water (thermal immersion suits are provided).
Torikatu 2, 914900 Kemi. Tel: (0) 16 256 548; www.sampotours.com

Lumilinna (Snow Castle)

Not quite as unique, but certainly unusual, is Lumilinna, the 'Snow Castle'. Not just the structure but also the seats, tables, etc., are made of ice, with suitable insulation such as reindeer hide provided where required. You can have a drink or a meal here, or stay in the ice hotel: needless to say, comfortable sleeping bags are provided! It is only open from late January to early April.
Torikatu 2, 94100 Kemi.
Tel: (0)16 259 502;
www.snowcastle.net

Northern Finland

Husky dogs

A ride on a husky-dog sled is one of the most enjoyable experiences of a Finnish winter. Husky-dog farms exist near most of the main winter resorts, and the dogs are used in racing as well as for tourist excursions.

There are several breeds of what aficionados call Northern Breed Dogs. However, purists insist that the only true Husky is the Siberian Husky. Originating from where the name suggests, the Siberian Husky was used for centuries by the Chukchi people for a range of tasks such as sled-pulling, reindeer-herding and guarding homesteads. The similar but slightly larger Alaskan Malamute, originating with the Malamute people (a tribe of Inuit) in Alaska, is often referred to as the Alaskan Husky.

Huskies are happiest when it is cold

There are claims that they have the wolf in their ancestry but these remain controversial, and the gentle nature of the Husky does not support them.

The Siberian Husky is surprisingly small, standing between 50 and 60cm (19½ and 23½ inches) at the shoulder and weighing from 16 to 27kg (35 to 60lb) – smaller than a Labrador. It is superbly adapted to its environment, with a soft outer coat over a very thick woolly undercoat. The broad paws have hair between the toes to aid grip on snow and ice. It is its eyes that many people find most striking, especially the ice-blue colour that is common in the breed. The eyes can also be amber or brown, and it is quite common for dogs to have one blue and one brown eye – referred to as being bi-eyed.

With their superb natural insulation and high-calorie diet, Huskies can live and work at temperatures down to at least −50°C (−58°F). In Finland they are normally kept outdoors all the year round, usually with a kennel to retreat to in very bad weather or when bearing pups. For these dogs, summer is the off-season. When cooler weather arrives, they need to be brought back into peak condition.

Their other qualities include speed and, above all, enormous stamina, strikingly demonstrated in the famous Iditarod race in Alaska, in which teams of 12 to 16 dogs cover 1,850km (1,150 miles) in 10 to 15 days. These dogs love to run. They will make a tremendous noise, barking and howling in excitement, when sleds are being prepared, but when they run they are almost silent. As any novice musher will discover, it is not getting them to go that is a problem but getting them to stop!

The dogs run in settled teams: when pulling light one- or two-person sleds for tourists, the teams consist of six to eight dogs. There is always a lead dog, who is often a female, as

Husky pups

female huskies tend to have a steadier temperament. At many farms visitors are allowed to 'mush' their own sleds: there is no need to be nervous as the dogs know what they are doing even if you don't!

Visitors on husky-dog sleds

Arktikum Museum

Rovaniemi

Rovaniemi is the northernmost point reached by most train services. One daily train continues a further 80km (50 miles) to Kemijärvi, but Rovaniemi is the hub from where bus services fan out over most of Lapland. This makes it at least a way station for many people, but there are several good reasons to linger for at least a night or two.

Rovaniemi stands by the impressive confluence of the rivers Oulasjoki and Kemijoki, the latter being the longest river in Finland (a little over 500km/ 311 miles), and also the last one (in 1991) to see logs being floated downstream in the time-honoured manner. The town was almost totally flattened by the retreating Germans in 1944, so all of it looks modern today. The central area was restored to a plan by Alvar Aalto. It was intended to resemble a reindeer's antlers, though this is far from obvious at ground level, and is not that evident even on a map.

Arktikum

A big attraction in the town is the splendid Arktikum: home of the Arctic Centre of the University of Lapland, it is an important focus of research into all things Arctic. It houses not one but two museums. The **Arctic Museum** presents all aspects of the region north of the Arctic Circle, from geological processes to wildlife and, above all, the traditional ways of life of the various indigenous peoples of the region. One cannot fail to be impressed, for instance, by the beauty and fragility of the various kayaks and by the aroma of the oils used to preserve their outer covers of hide.

Across the hall is the **Provincial Museum of Lapland**, which provides a background to life in the region, employing artefacts, multimedia and some fine tableaux. These are much better than average, and the stuffed animals look incredibly lifelike.

The building itself, designed by a Danish partnership, is extremely striking and has become something of a symbol of the town: it has even been copied, after a fashion, in one of the town-centre shopping malls. The emblematic glass-roofed atrium is an impressive 172m (188yds) long. Inside it is largely empty: the exhibition areas are underground, flanking the atrium.

There is a museum shop, with a far more tasteful range of products than are available at most local tourist outlets, and a nice café.
Pohjoisranta 4. Tel: (0) 16 322 3260; www.arktikum.fi.
Open: daily summer, rest of the year Tue–Sun. Admission charge.

What Rovaniemi also has on offer is lots of shopping: it is a good place to look for Lappish souvenirs (note that items produced by genuine *Sámi* craftworkers carry the Sámi Duodji label). And there is a clutch of Alvar Aalto buildings around the modest civic plaza, including the town hall, library and **Lappia-talo**, the town's theatre and concert venue (*Jorma Etontie 8a, 96100 Rovaniemi; tel: (0) 16 356 2096; www.rovaniemi.fi/teatteri; by appointment or to attend a performance*).

Santa Claus

The real reason why people come to Rovaniemi is because of Santa Claus, who has his office here about 8km (5 miles) north of the town, bang on the Arctic Circle (*see pp137–8*). There is a Santa Claus Hotel, a Santa Claus Tourist Office, even a Santa Technology Park. Another point in Rovaniemi's favour is that it is a year-round place. You will find that outdoor activities are available in September and October, a rarity in other Finnish centres.

ROVANIEMI ENVIRONS

The big draw in Rovaniemi actually lies 8km (5 miles) or so outside the town, where the main highway north crosses the Arctic Circle – Napapiiri in Finnish. Here you will find no fewer than three petrol stations with attendant cafés and souvenir shops, but they are really hanging on to the coat-tails of the great man himself, whose HQ is just across the highway. There are regular buses there from the town, or you could rent a bike – it is not far and you will be able to tell your friends that you cycled across the Arctic Circle.

Santa Claus Village (Joulupukin Pajakylä)

Santa Claus Village (Joulupukin Pajakylä) is corny but at the same time strangely engaging. You can meet Santa in his workshop and have your photo taken with him – by the time you've finished your chat and entered your name in his atlas (so he'll know where to come next time), the print will be ready. Anyone who is still young at heart will love it. And cynics can always try and catch Santa in an inconsistency (they won't succeed).

There is no admission charge to enter the village but you do have to pay to have your photo taken with Santa. Santa's Office is open all the year: ask him how he can manage to be here and still deliver all those presents around the world and he will explain that there is something magical about time beyond the Arctic Circle. *96930 Napapiiri. Tel: (0) 16 356 2096;*

www.santaclausvillage.info.
Open: all year. Free admission.

In the same complex is **Santa Claus' Main Post Office**. You can send ordinary postcards here and get a special postmark, or of course buy special cards and letter forms (*96930 Napapiiri; tel: (0) 204 523 120; www.posti.fi/postimerkkikeskus/jpp/ en_index.html; open: daily*).

Around and about are cafés, restaurants and souvenir shops. Be careful of the array of tacky, mass-produced rubbish on sale, and take a look at the genuine

The 'real' Santa Claus Village

local hand-crafted merchandise instead.

Nearby is Santa Park (*see p164*), which is a small theme park, and a big hit with youngsters.

Ounasvaara Ski Centre

Even closer to the town centre, within walking distance, is the Ounasvaara ski centre. It has 7 runs, 4 lifts and around 100km (62 miles) of cross-country tracks. There is a summer toboggan run, and you can take a lift up to view the wide scenery and the two great rivers.
Taunontie 14, 96600 Rovaniemi.
Tel: (0) 16 369 045;
www.ounasvaara.net/Hiihtokeskus/
English/frontpage.htm

Ranua Zoo

About 80km (50 miles) south and reachable by bus, is the Ranua Zoo, which houses nearly all of Finland's important wild species in a reasonably natural setting. While there are plenty of other places to see reindeer, encounters with elk, bears or eagles are a lot less likely to happen elsewhere. The enclosures are well spread out through natural woodland, which is populated by red squirrels.
Rovaniementie 29, 97700 Ranua. Tel: (0) 16 355 1921; www.ranuazoo.com. Open: daily, summer longer hours. Admission charge.

Kuusamo

The Kuusamo region is one of the leading areas in Finland for outdoor

activities of all kinds, at any time of the year. It is top of the list for adrenalin junkies, but there is plenty of relaxed fare on offer too, with some of Finland's finest walking and trekking trails.

Kuusamo town is the main regional centre, and the airport is just a few kilometres south. It is a pleasant even if not dramatic town, and it is well endowed with companies offering outdoor activities and tours. There is also a very well-equipped information centre on the outskirts, right by the main road, which should be the first port of call for anyone arriving without a clear schedule. Steer clear of the rather mystical audio-visual show which is unlikely to leave you any wiser: a more productive use of time would be to concentrate on the maps, displays and quizzing the knowledgeable and enthusiastic staff.

THE STORY OF SANTA CLAUS

It is widely believed that the name Santa Claus derives from St Nicholas, from 4th-century Asia Minor, a protector of children and a charitable figure. Elements from pagan folk myths were undoubtedly incorporated later. His Finnish name is Joulupukki: *Joulu* has the same root as 'Yule' while *pukki* means 'billy-goat' or 'buck'.

It is only Santa's Office that you can visit: his home is further north and its location is secret. Many Finns maintain that he lives in a mountain in remote Lapland called Korvatunturi or 'Ear Mountain', its ear-like shape allowing Santa to hear the wishes of children from far away.

Hannu Hautala Nature Photography Centre

Next door to the Tourist Information centre is this brand-new centre celebrating the life's work of Finland's most famous nature photographer (born 1941). As Finland's first centre dedicated to nature photography, it also shows outstanding work from other practitioners.

Torangintaival 2, 93600 Kuusamo. Tel: (0) 4 0860 8364; www.hannuhautala.fi. Open: daily in summer. Admission charge, free for children under 7.

Ruka

Ruka, about 25km (15^1/$_2$ miles) north of Kuusamo, is one of Finland's major ski centres. It is not as extensive as Ylläs but has some steeper slopes, and is particularly popular with snowboarders and freestyle skiers. Like any ski area in Finland, there are plenty of gentler slopes for the novice as well, especially on the eastern face of the fell.

Ruka village is not particularly attractive (its focal point is a car park!) but it has the advantage of being right at the foot of the main lift.

Ruka is also a good base for a wide range of year-round outdoor activities: several safari companies operate from the village. Snowmobile excursions are popular – but watch out for the spoof Russian border posts! As a cross-country ski centre, it is good, though perhaps not on a par with Ylläs or Saariselkä.

In summer Ruka is quieter but there is still plenty going on. There are fine hiking opportunities – it is one of the end points of the highly regarded Karhunkierros trail – and it is also a good place for mountain-biking. Unless you have a beefed-up bike and body armour, you probably won't want to attempt the downhill course (accessed by ski lift), but you can ride some of the gentler slopes or wander off into the forests.

Oulanka National Park

Another 40km (25 miles) north you come to the southern boundary of Oulanka National Park, one of Finland's most popular wilderness areas. Its forested fells are seamed by fast-flowing rivers, which have carved out some fine gorges. There are abundant possibilities for hiking, rafting or canoeing. A larger number of operators are based in Ruka and Kuusamo, but a few companies can be found within the park as well. There is an information centre on the way to the park which can advise on hiking and other activities. As with any northern hiking area, the *ruska* (autumn) season is a good time to visit.

Salla

The small town of Salla lies 100km (62 miles) north of Kuusamo, and about 30km (18^1/$_2$ miles) beyond the Arctic Circle. The present Russian border lies only a few kilometres to the east, and a large slice of Finnish

Oulanka National Park

territory was lost after the Second World War, causing considerable displacement of population. However, Salla seems to have recovered well. It is a thriving centre with a small downhill ski centre and some good cross-country trails. More interestingly, it is one of the places where you can find traces of the *Sámi* (Lapp) tradition.

Sallan Poropuisto (Reindeer Farm)
It is also home to a large and well-run reindeer farm, Sallan Poropuisto. You can see the reindeer at close quarters and may join in their feeding. There is also a fine exhibition on the local environment, and on the life of reindeer and their herders.

Other activities you can access here include: sleeping in a traditional peat hut, taking a sleigh ride, learning to walk with snowshoes, or enjoying a week's safari travelling by a mix of dog-sleds, reindeer sleighs and on your own feet (in snowshoes).
Hautajärventie 111, 98900 Salla
Tel: (0) 16 837 771;
http://matkailu.salla.fi/?deptid=16761

Kittilä
Kittilä is the main regional centre in the northwest. It is not particularly tourist-oriented but its airport makes it an obvious transit point on the way to Levi or Ylläs. Both have the usual range of summer activities, but come into their own especially in winter.

Walk: Pieni Karhunkierros Trail

Pieni Karhunkierros means 'Little Bear's Trail', as distinct from the Karhunkierros, which is an 80km (50-mile) trek, typically expected to take 4 or 5 days. Pieni Karhunkierros is a much easier proposition, but still takes in a large slice of Finnish wilderness, with rocky gorges, tumbling rapids and colourful mires along the way. The route is well marked and there are duckboards at many tricky sections, especially where it is swampy; wearing proper boots is strongly recommended.

Time: 2½ or 4½ hours depending on whether the shortcut back is taken. Distance: 6 or 12km (3³/4 or 7½ miles).

The actual walking time is likely to be around 4–5 hours, but with so many spectacular sights along the way, as well as several shelters or cabins where you can stop for a break, it is worth allowing for extra time. There is a shortcut which halves both distance and time. Start at Juuma (accessible by bus from Kuusamo and Ruka). The trail begins where the road ends. There's a café and information point. You'll cross the Kitka river several times during the walk and it's worth looking out for rafting parties at any of the crossings. If you decide you'd like a go, there's a rafting company, Kitka Safaris, right by the car park.
Follow the well-marked opening section, with lots of duckboards, to a suspension bridge poised over Niskakoski rapids. Continue through forest, climbing gently and then descending.

1 Myllykoski

Myllykoski simply means 'mill rapids' so it's hardly a surprise to find an old watermill here, which has now been restored. Nearby is a firepit, which is available for the use of all hikers. Just beyond is a suspension bridge giving a great view of the rapids and the mill. *Cross the bridge and follow the path to Pyöreälampi.*

2 Pyöreälampi

This pretty little tarn is another tempting place to linger. There are fireplaces, a woodpile, and a 'long-drop' toilet. It all exemplifies the Finnish approach, embracing the wilderness but not neglecting the basic comforts.
The trail winds past pools and mires, with duckboards wherever it would otherwise be too wet, before a short climb to Kallioportti.

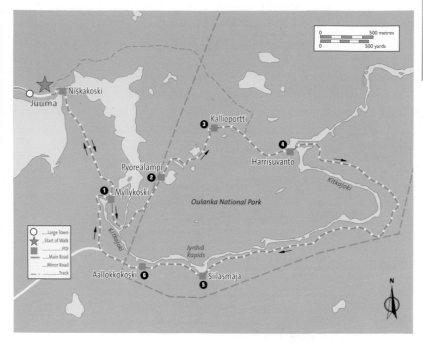

3 Kallioportti

This is a fantastic viewpoint, poised above steep cliffs. The deep hollow is part of a gorge system carved by mighty rivers at the end of the last ice age but now occupied only by a tiny stream. *Descend a long wooden staircase then follow the stream to a suspension bridge. (The shortcut back to Juuma goes left soon after the descent.)*

4 Harrisuvanto

There is yet another campfire site and lean-to shelter just before the bridge. Spanning 50m (55yds), this is the longest bridge on the route, but the river below is much more placid. You soon begin to get spectacular views of a long gorge, around 60m (200ft) deep.

Cross the bridge and follow the trail, swinging right and climbing gradually. The trail then runs along the edge of the gorge before descending to Siilasmaja.

5 Siilasmaja

Here you'll find another campfire and a cosy cabin, but everything is dominated by the thundering rapids of Jyrävä. *Climb up past the rapids and continue along the path.*

6 Aallokkokoski

These rapids are in complete contrast to Jyrävä, stretching over almost 1km (²/₃ mile). For rafters these represent the highlight of the trip. *Keep to the right at the next junction and it's only a short way back to Myllykoski.*

Reindeer

The Eurasian 'reindeer' and the North American 'caribou' are in fact the same species of large deer, its Latin name being *Rangifer tarandus*. In North America many caribou are wild, but in Finland, as in Norway and Sweden, all reindeer are owned and managed by someone. Reindeer herding was traditionally a mainstay of economic life for much of northern Finland, notably but not exclusively for the *Sámi* people.

A reindeer at Salla

Today few people depend on the reindeer exclusively, but it is still an important source of income. There are around 7,000 registered reindeer owners; between them they are responsible for over 200,000 animals.

Vast tracts of northern Finland are designated as reindeer husbandry areas, amounting to 114,000sq km (44,000sq miles) or around a third of the total area of the country. Owners are represented by 57 local associations and jointly by the National Federation of Reindeer Herding Associations. Reindeer numbers are limited by the Ministry of Agriculture and Forestry, to ensure that the population remains at a sustainable level. However, in some areas the demand for timber has led to conflict between logging interests and reindeer herding. While Finnish forests are sustainable in that replacement planting takes place, the lichens on which the reindeer depend for much of their diet are very slow to regenerate.

Reindeer are different from other deer in a number of ways, especially in the ways they adapt to the Arctic environment. Their thick coat is one obvious feature; then there are the broad hooves, which are spread to

Watchful reindeer

distribute the animal's weight. This is useful for negotiating swamps in summer and snow in winter.

Both sexes have antlers. The males use theirs in competition for mates, while the females use theirs mainly to protect their young ones against predators, of which the most dangerous is the wolf. Wolves are a menace to reindeer in Finland, especially in the east where they frequently cross the border from Russia.

The importance of the reindeer in traditional northern Finnish life cannot be overstated. They were used to pull sleds, and to provide milk as well as meat. When an animal was slaughtered, almost every part of it was put to some use. The skin, with its excellent insulating properties, was used for tents and clothes. The properties of the skin are so good that reindeer-skin clothes are still used today. The tendons and sinews were made into thread, and the antlers – shed annually – were used to make knives and other implements.

While traditionally reindeer were herded throughout the year, today they are left to their own devices for much of the time. Snowmobiles are now used to herd scattered reindeer. Groups of reindeer can often be seen at the roadside in the husbandry area, but the best way to get close to these fascinating creatures and to learn more about them is to visit a reindeer farm, where the animals are kept within a relatively small range. Visitors can see the reindeer at close quarters and may be able to participate in feeding or even take a ride behind one in a traditional sled.

Cross-country skiing at Ylläs

Levi

Levi is reckoned to have some of Finland's best après-ski, along with the country's only gondola lift. The skiing is good, too. However, Levi has more of a brash commercial air than most Finnish resorts. However it is always possible to escape fairly quickly into untrammelled nature.

There is a summer toboggan run and all the usual outdoor activities. In summer, you can also take a mountain bike up on the lifts.

Tel: (0) 16 639 3300; www.levi.fi

Ylläs

Ylläs is rated alongside Ruka as one of the best ski areas in Finland for both downhill and cross-country, and if you want to sample both there is no better destination.

The downhill skiing is on both sides of the bald **Yllästunturi**, the highest skiing hill in Finland. There are 43 runs – the most in any resort in Finland – with 21 lifts and tows. Not only does

Ylläs offer the longest downhill runs in the country (3,000m/9,840ft with a drop of 463m/1,520ft), it also has incredibly expansive views from the upper slopes.

The one thing it lacks is steepness. This makes it a tame proposition for the expert skier but a flattering one for the intermediate – even its 'black' runs would be no more than ordinary 'red' runs in the Alps. With its wealth of gentle, broad runs and reliable snow conditions, it is an excellent place to learn to ski. Most of the instructors speak excellent English, too.

If the downhill skiing is good, the cross-country is outstanding, probably vying with Saariselkä for the title of the best in Finland. There are 320km (199 miles) of groomed trails, dotted with 'wilderness cafés' where you can warm up with a *kahvi* or something stronger.

Ylläsjärvi and Äkäslompolo

There are two villages at the foot of the fell – Ylläsjärvi to the south and

Äkäslompolo to the north. Ylläsjärvi is more of a custom-built resort, handy if you just want to ski but rather soulless otherwise; Äkäslompolo is much more of a real place. Alternative activities like husky-dog sledding or reindeer farm visits can easily be arranged from both places.

Ylläs Ski Oy Finland, Äkäsentie 10, 95970 Ylläs/Äkäslompolo. Tel: (0) 16 553 000; www.yllas.fi

Ivalo

As the northernmost airport on the domestic network, Ivalo is an obvious destination for those who want to experience the far north. However, most travellers end up bypassing the town itself and heading either south about 25km (16 miles) to Saariselkä or north almost 40km (25 miles) to Inari. *(Buses to/from Saariselkä connect with every flight, those to Inari are less frequent.)*

The E75 highway continues further north. Although the loss of the Petsamo area means Finland no longer has a foothold on the Arctic Sea, you can continue through to Finnmark in northern Norway. The common *Sámi* culture ensures strong ties across the border.

Ivalo itself is not a great tourist centre, but it is convenient because of its airport. It also makes a good base for anyone planning a trip into Lemmenjoki National Park, Finland's largest, and home to some of its most dramatic scenery. If you have access to

a car, it is easy to head on up to Inari, stopping off here and there to take in some of the wonderful views over **Inarijärvi (Lake Inari)**. This is the largest lake in Arctic Finland, though it is so cut into by peninsulas and sprinkled with islands that it is hard to get a sense of its true scale. You can also take a cruise on the broad Ivalo river (cruises go from right behind Hotel Ivalo, so enquire here).

Saariselkä

Saariselkä is the main tourist centre in this vast region. You are unlikely to be bowled over by the beauty of the town itself, though it is pleasant enough, but it is surrounded by vast tracts of mostly empty fells. Just to the east is the boundary of the Urho Kekkonen National Park, the second largest National Park in Finland, and one of its most revered wilderness areas. Saariselkä offers a wide choice of outdoor activities, in both winter and summer. It is not a bad place to start

CROSS-COUNTRY SKIING

Cross-country skiing might appear strenuous, but in fact – at least on level trails – it is as easy or hard as you choose to make it. Almost everywhere in Finland, throughout the long winter, a network of trails is prepared and regularly groomed. The 'skinny' skis and soft boots, which can be hired in most centres, are infinitely more comfortable than the hard downhill boots, and cheaper too. While most people can strap skis on their feet and make some progress on a level track right away, a few hours' tuition is recommended.

discovering something of the *Sámi* (Lapp) tradition, though Inari is a better bet for this. A more unusual attraction in the vicinity is gold-mining, and the chance to try your hand at gold-panning.

The Tourist Information Centre and several service providers are located in the Siula centre, just off the main highway; buses stop outside.
Information Centre. Tel: (0) 16 668 402; www.saariselka.fi. Open: Mon–Fri 9am–5pm.

Urho Kekkonen National Park

Also known as Koilliskaira, or more familiarly as UKK (Kansallispuisto is Finnish for National Park), Urho Kekkonen National Park encompasses 255,000 hectares (630,120 acres) of rolling fell country. The tree line is low here and the tops are bare and often windswept, offering almost limitless horizons. The intervening valleys, threaded by rivers, are mostly forested, the dominant species being the Scots pine and birch. It is a haven for wild beasts, with bears and wolverines lurking in the deeper reaches, and wolves are sighted regularly. It is also home to more than 20,000 reindeer which, though not strictly wild, roam free for most of the year.

While the deeper reaches of the park are strictly for the dedicated hiker, fine shorter walks are available. In winter, you can go in snowshoes: any of the numerous safari companies in town will organise it, and you can pick up the

rudiments of the technique very quickly. Several trails start from the edge of Saariselkä town itself.

For a slightly longer walk, a popular destination is the wilderness hut near the unexpected little gorge of Rumakuru. You can pick up an excellent map of the trails for a few euros from the Siula centre in Saariselkä.

All the usual outdoor activities are available in or near Saariselkä, where at least half a dozen safari companies compete for business. In summer and autumn there are guided trekking trips into UKK, while in areas outside the park, you can go mountain-biking, kayaking or fishing. In winter you can be guided into the white wilderness in snowshoes or on cross-country skis, and outside the National Park there are also husky and reindeer safaris, snowmobile trips and much more.

It is unlikely that anyone would travel from overseas just for Saariselkä's downhill skiing. But anyone who is in the area and fancies a day on the slopes will find a fair amount to try out, with ten slopes spread across two fells. The longest run is 1,300m (4,265ft) with a drop of about 180m (590ft). And you will be able to say that you've skied the world's most northerly resort. It also has Finland's longest toboggan run, just a shade shorter than the longest ski run.

For cross-country skiing, on the other hand, Saariselkä is an excellent venue, with 240km (149 miles) of maintained trails. Of these, 34km (21 miles) are illuminated during the dark days of midwinter, and you can always take a headtorch for the rest. Those who have experienced it wax lyrical about gliding silently along under the glow of the Northern Lights. It is even easier under a full moon, which shines so brightly off the snow that no torch is needed.

Tankavaara

About 30km (18^1/2 miles) south of Saariselkä and served by several buses daily, Tankavaara is home to the **Gold Prospector Museum**, which sets out to illustrate what was, and for a rugged few still is, a tough and lonely way of life. Of course what everyone wants to do is to try it for themselves, and everything you need is available along with guidance in the correct technique. And who's to say you will not strike lucky?
99695 Tankavaara. Tel: (0) 16 626 171;
www.kultamuseo.fi

Inari

Like most towns in northern Lapland, most of Inari was badly damaged in the war and it has been rebuilt from scratch, rather gracelessly, it must be said, and with little effort to capitalise on its grand situation on the shores of the Inarijärvi.

However, Inari is one of the main centres for the *Sámi* culture and, as home to the marvellous **Siida Museum**, it is pretty much the best place to go to learn about the *Sámi*. There is the usual itinerary of outdoor activities, and here, too, you can go gold-panning. There is

also a wonderful walk to the lovely little **Wilderness Church** (*see pp150–51*).

Inari is about 40km (25 miles) north of Ivalo and there are a few buses both ways every day, so you can make a day trip. But if you want to take in a lake cruise or the walk to the Wilderness Church, the schedules don't really allow enough time. In that case the options are either to spend a night in Inari, or to take a taxi at least one way.

Siida

Siida is the great attraction in Inari, and well worth travelling a long way for. Housed in a fine new building, it is both a museum of *Sámi* life and culture and a nature centre, reflecting the inextricable dependence of the traditional *Sámi* way of life on the natural environment.

The indoor halls are only one half of Siida: outside is an extensive open-air museum, which pre-dates the new building by several decades. This site has yielded the earliest evidence of human habitation in northern Lapland, dating back 9,000 years. Scattered through the trees are examples of both relatively recent homes, inhabited until the 1950s, and structures used by the *Sámi* in their nomadic past. These include everything from sleeping shelters to beartraps.
Siida, 99870 Inari.
Tel: (0) 16 665 212; www.siida.fi.
Open: June–Sept daily 9am–8pm,
Oct–May Tue–Sun 10am–5pm.
Admission charge.

Walk: Inari Wilderness Church

The Wilderness Church (Erämaäkirkko) by the lake of Pielpajärvi stands on a site long used as a Sámi meeting place. The first church here was built in the 17th century, and the present structure dates from the years 1752–60. It is still used for worship, usually at Easter and midsummer. It is also occasionally used for weddings. It is a simple but beautiful building, made entirely of wood, and a very evocative spot if you are lucky enough to have it to yourself.

The journey is as attractive as the destination, passing through beautiful forests and skirting several lakes. At *ruska* time, the displays of colours can be almost beyond belief.

You can walk to the church from Inari but the first 2.5km (1¹/₂ miles) are out of keeping with the rest, following a road which, though quiet, has none of the beauty or interest of the rest of the trail. If you have your own transport, it is easy to reach the start of the walk proper, while a popular strategy is to hire a bike from the Inari Info centre.

The official distance for the 'real' walk is 4.5km (2³/₄ miles) each way, but judging from unofficial amendments to the sign at the start, many feel that it's a bit longer! It is certainly advisable to allow three hours for the 9km (5¹/₂-mile) walk, plus time that may be spent admiring the scenery, or lost in contemplation at the church.

The route is described starting from Inari Info.
Whether by car or bike, or on foot, follow the main road northward past Siida. Immediately after, turn right on Sariniementie. Follow the tarmac surface which gives way to a dirt track, for about 2.5km (1¹/₂ miles). Note that the first sign for 'Wilderness Church' leaving the road is in fact a cross-country ski route: bogs and lakes make it impassable in summer. Continue to a parking area.

1 Car park

There are toilet facilities here. Bikes and cars should be left at this point. The track from here follows an undulating course through tall pine woods. There are many huge boulders scattered around, left by retreating ice sheets. The forest floor is thickly carpeted with lichens, known as an indicator of both clean air and lack of disturbance.

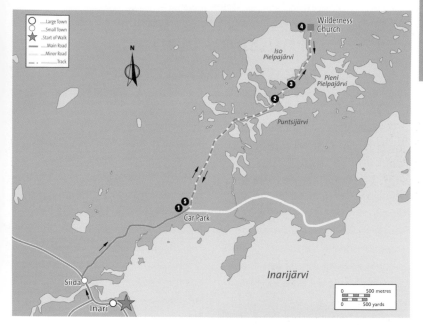

Follow the obvious track from the corner of the car park. The track passes several small lakes or tarns, but the first to be recognised by a sign is Puntsijärvi. Continue a short distance to another lake, on the right.

2 Pieni Pielpajärvi

Soon after this you come to the reedy shores of Pieni (small) Pielpajärvi, on the right.

Keep on the path until another lake appears on the left.

3 Iso Pielpajärvi

Iso (great) Pielpajärvi comes into view on the left. Although it is not huge, Iso Pielpajärvi does give a sense of space rare on this walk. The track now negotiates a narrow isthmus between the two lakes, with alternating glimpses of both. Arrive at a small cabin, originally used to accommodate parishioners who had travelled great distances.

The forest opens out, and the path forks. Take the right fork, passing a small raised barn, to get the first view of the church.

4 Wilderness Church

In this isolated spot the priests would have had to fend for themselves to a large extent, aided by offerings from parishioners.

Return by the same route.

5 Rocky knoll

At the end, scramble up the rocky knoll overlooking the car park to view Inari village to the south.

The *Sámi* (Lapps): people and culture

The origins of the *Sámi* people are somewhat uncertain. It is likely that they share a common ancestry with the Finns; their language certainly belongs to the same family (Finno-Ugrian), but seems to have begun to diverge more than 2,000 years ago. Subsequently the *Sámi* developed in isolation, not only from other peoples but even from each other, so that many distinct subcultures evolved, along with their own distinct dialects.

The area known generally as Lapland, but more correctly as Sapmi, stretches across northern Norway, Sweden and the Kola Peninsula in Russia, as well as northern Finland. The total population of *Sámi* is around 75,000, of whom by far the greatest number live in Norway. There are around 7,500 *Sámi* in Finland, and even in most areas of 'Lapland' they are now outnumbered by Finns. The most strongly *Sámi* municipality in Finland is Utsjoki, about 100km (62 miles) north of Inari.

The common image of the *Sámi* as nomadic reindeer herders is not false, but needs some qualification. Throughout their history, many *Sámi* populations, such as those around Inari, had a more diverse form of livelihood in which fishing was a primary occupation. Hunting was also important, and in fact the *Sámi* were reindeer hunters long before they became herders. It is probable that the use of a tame animal as a decoy was the first step towards herding them. Their completely

Siida Sámi Museum, Inari

Sámi crafts

no longer the same need to travel with the herds.

Traditional *Sámi* beliefs closely centred on nature. The leader of the community was the shaman, who would go into a trance by beating a drum and could then communicate with the gods. In the 17th century the *Sámi* were forcibly converted to Christianity. The shaman's drum was seen as a potent symbol of paganism, and most were destroyed. Those that survived only did so by being collected for museums far from Sapmi. Today most *Sámi* are nominally Lutheran, but the group known as *Skolt Sámi* are Eastern Orthodox, having been relocated from the Petsamo region, when it was annexed by the then Soviet Union.

Reindeer husbandry is still a major source of income for around 40 per cent of the *Sámi*. An almost equal number now work in modern service industries, while a significant number make their living from traditional handicraft products. By tradition, men work with wood and reindeer horn, while women concentrate on leather and cloth.

nomadic way of life, in which the people followed the reindeer on their migration, was severely restricted in the 19th century by the closure of national borders, leading to the development of the system still used today, where the reindeer roam extensively but within defined boundaries (which is why the traveller in Lapland occasionally comes across tall fences stretching as far as the eye can see). Today, with the use of motorbikes or snowmobiles, there is

To identify genuine *Sámi* craft products, look for the *Sámi duodji* label. This is issued by the Sámi Handicraft Association of Finland. A parallel scheme of identification also operates in Sweden and Norway.

Getting away from it all

A large country with a small population, Finland is an ideal getaway. You can rent a country cottage or stay in a rural B&B; head out to the islands of the Turku Archipelago or Åland; or spend a day or longer hiking or trekking in the vast spaces of Finland's northern fells. If you don't have much time at hand, go to a National Park: there are 35 such parks in Finland, so there's always one within easy reach, like Nuuksio, which is readily accessible from Helsinki.

Seasons

It is not just a matter of where to go but when. Many of Finland's resorts and attractions still have a very short season: places that are only open from Midsummer until the end of August. The same is true for popular outings such as lake cruises. If all you want is peace and quiet, visiting Finland off-season can be great, but check first to make sure accommodation is available.

NORDIC WALKING

At first sight, Nordic walking is simply walking with a couple of adjustable poles, similar to ski-sticks. In fact, there is a definite technique to it, which is easily picked up within a short period of instruction (an hour is plenty for most people). It is similar, but not identical, to the use of the arms in cross-country skiing.

Using the poles correctly reduces the load on knees and ankles. It also allows walkers to give the upper body a gentle workout, making it a highly effective form of all-round exercise.

Hiking

The Midsummer–August pattern does not apply everywhere, however, and in many of the main hiking areas, especially in the north, one of the most popular times to visit is autumn, when the days are crisp and cool and the *ruska* colours are at their height. If you're lucky you may even catch a glimpse of the Northern Lights in the evening. All the main services are active in these areas at this time.

Archipelago National Park

The main centres of the Turku and Åland Archipelagos are described (see *pp82–3 and 96–9*), but if you want to escape your fellow humans, it is hard to do better than head for one of the smaller outlying islands. For instance, Aspö, Nötö and Jurmo, served by a ferry from Turku (*departures June–mid-Aug Mon and Thur*), are all within the Archipelago National Park and have places to stay.

MOKKI

Thousands of city-dwelling Finns own a *mokki*, or summer cottage, an ideal base for getting back to nature. There are 30,000 of them around the shores of Lake Saimaa alone. And Finns take this back-to-nature thing pretty seriously. The ideal *mokki* stands in a forest close to a lake or river, and it is a pretty simple structure. In many cases it is a plain wooden cabin, sometimes without electricity or even running water. It is certainly more likely to have a sauna than a shower.

The actual *mokki* is very much a family affair and unless you have Finnish friends you are unlikely to have access to one. The cottages that are rented out to visitors are usually equipped more sophisticatedly.

RIGHT OF ACCESS ('EVERY MAN'S RIGHT')

Jokamiehenoikeus (Swedish: *Allemansratt*) is usually translated as 'every man's right', though, naturally, it applies to women too! This long-established tradition gives everyone the right to walk almost anywhere, including on private property, and to travel in other low-impact ways, such as on skis or by canoe. It also includes the right to pick berries and mushrooms. On public land you may also light a fire or pitch a tent for one night: on private land, the owner's permission is required. Tighter restrictions sometimes apply in national parks and conservation areas. For more details see: *www.luontoon.fi/page.asp?section=5800*

Getting away from it all

The accommodation is limited, however, and it would be rash to arrive without booking ahead. Other islands have no scheduled ferry service and unless you have your own boat you will have to rely on the boat-taxi services that operate in the area.

The main Turku Archipelago

Outside the summer season, even the main Turku Archipelago is wonderfully quiet. September is the ideal time to go, especially if you're cycling, but it can be quite magical in winter too.

Private islands

Some of the private islands have isolated cottages that you can rent. Lomarengas, for instance, lists around 20 of them (*see p175*).

Uninhabited islands

Camping on an uninhabited island must be one of the ultimate ways to escape, and will appeal to anyone who ever loved *Robinson Crusoe* or *Swallows and Amazons*. On several of the islands in the National Park there are campfire sites, accessible by your own boat or canoe, or by arrangement with a boat-taxi service.

The Turku Archipelago: islands in a glittering sea

Shopping

Finland's high standard of living is reflected in the range and quality of goods available in its shops, but cheap it is not. For most goods, the prices are broadly comparable to British levels, which means that North American visitors are likely to find it expensive. Finland certainly is not a place for bargains on consumer electronics – not even Nokia mobile phones!

What to buy

It is worth taking advantage of Finland's exceptional strength in the fields of art and design to seek out original and high-quality goods: from paintings and drawings to weaving, glass or jewellery, and distinctive traditional crafts from Karelia or Lapland.

In summer, browsing in the open-air markets is a good way to find fine work on offer at reasonable prices, and you'll often get to meet the artist too. There are concentrations of craft workers in towns like Porvoo and Fiskars, but almost anywhere you go in Finland you will find distinctive and original work on sale. It is surprising how often you come across genuine hand-crafted products while waiting for a flight at a small regional airport, for instance.

Several of the stores listed below are represented at Helsinki's Vantaa airport for those last-minute purchases. Stockmann has an outlet there, selling Finnish foods, general souvenirs, and Aarika and Iittala products.

Where to buy

HELSINKI

Aarika

Aarika offers eye-catching wooden jewellery and other gifts.
Pohjoesplanadi 27, and throughout Finland.

Artek

Artek, established by Alvar and Aino Aalto, mainly sells furniture, but also a wide range of lamps.
Eteläesplanadi 18, 00130 Helsinki.
Tel: (0) 9 6132 5277.
Many other outlets also.

Design District Helsinki

The area known as the Design District stretches southwest from the Esplanade and includes dozens of designer shops, galleries and museums, with plenty of cafés, bars and restaurants.
Design Forum Finland. Erottajankatu 7, 00130 Helsinki. Tel: (0) 9 6220 8132; www.designforum.fi/ designforumfinland_en.

Iittala

Iittala produces distinctive glassware and ceramics, including designs by Aino and Alvar Aalto.
Pohjoisesplanadi 25, 00100 Helsinki.
Tel: (0) 204 39 3501.
Many other outlets also.

Kalevala Koru

Kalevala Koru jewellery features unmistakably Finnish motifs, including elements from the *Kalevala* in gold, silver and bronze.
Unioninkatu 25, 00170 Helsinki.
Tel: (0) 207611 380.
Many other outlets also.

Marimekko

Marimekko is well known for colourful fabrics, clothing and bags.
Eteläesplanadi 14, 00130 Helsinki.
Tel: (0) 9 170 704.
Stores in Turku, Tampere and several other cities.

Shopping Centre Kamppi

Home to 150 shops and restaurants.
Urho Kekkosen katu 1, 00100 Helsinki.
Tel: (0) 9 742 98552;
www.kamppi.fi/english

Stockmann

Stockmann department stores, notably in central Helsinki, sell just about everything.
Aleksanterinkatu 52, B 00100 Helsinki.
Tel: (0) 9 121 3638; www.stockmann.fi

There is a large Stockmann store in **Itäkeskus**, easily reached by Metro.
Itäkatu 1 C, 00930 Helsinki.
Tel: (0) 9 121 461; www.stockmann.fi

Naantali

Moominshop

Moominshop in Naantali is devoted, naturally, to all things Moomin.
Mannerheiminkatu 3, Naantali.
Tel: (0) 2 511 1120.

Find some unusual jewellery at Kalevala Koru

Entertainment

Perhaps it is because of the need to fill the long winter nights, but Finland certainly has plenty of entertainment of all kinds at all times of the year, with a fair proportion of it moving outdoors in summer. Music occupies the primary place, and there is an abundance of it, especially classical and jazz. The rich line-up of festivals is mentioned on pp24–5, but there are many year-round venues.

Classical music

Finlandia Hall

Helsinki's Finlandia Hall is home to both the Helsinki Philharmonic Orchestra and the Finnish Radio Symphony Orchestra. It also hosts international visiting orchestras and other artists like Kiri Te Kanawa.
Mannerheimintie 13e, 00100 Helsinki.
Tel: (0) 9 402 41;
www.finlandiatalo.fi/en

The Opera House

Opera also receives a lot of support, with the Savonlinna Festival and Finnish National Opera in Helsinki leading the way.

All operas are staged in their original language, and subtitles are provided in Finnish and English.

Besides opera, the Opera House in Helsinki stages classical ballet and contemporary dance, and has its own ballet school. It also hosts a variety of music concerts including jazz.
Helsinginkatu 58, 00251 Helsinki.

Tel: (0) 9 403 02 211; www.operafin.fi

Sibelius Hall

Finland's leading orchestra is the Lahti Sinfonia, under conductor Osmo Vänskä. Its home is the magnificent Sibelius Hall, an architectural and acoustic masterpiece, which hosts performances of opera and other musical genres.
Ankkurikatu 7, 15140 Lahti.
Tel: (0) 38 142 800; www.sibeliustalo.fi

TANGO

Finland has a particular obsession with the tango, the present enthusiasm for it possibly even exceeding that of Argentina, where the dance form originated in the early 20th century. Within a short time the tango became immensely popular all over Europe. One reason for its continuing popularity in Finland is perhaps that composers found it compatible with older Finnish melodies.

One can go so far as to say that the tango capital of the world today is not Buenos Aires but Seinajoki, a small town about four hours from Helsinki, which hosts an annual tango festival.

A French horn player in a Helsinki brass band

Other cities in Finland with professional orchestras are **Joensuu**, **Jyväskylä**, **Kuopio**, **Kotka/Kouvola**, **Lappeenranta**, **Oulu**, **Pori**, **Tampere**, **Espoo Turku** and **Vaasa**. There are also many chamber orchestras and semi-professional ensembles.

Jazz

It is said that jazz was brought to Finland by a group of American musicians in 1926, and it has had a strong hold ever since. The Pori Festival of jazz is internationally renowned (*see p24*).

HELSINKI
Happy Jazz Club Storyville
Live jazz virtually every night, with Cajun-Creole food.

Museokatu 8.
Tel: (0) 9 408 007.
Admission charge.

TAMPERE
Flat Note Jazz Club
Live jazz of all kinds every night, and good food to go with it.
Kuninkaankatu 1.
Tel: (0) 40 517 6290.
Open Tue–Sat.

TURKU
Harlem Jazz Club
A long-established jazz club.
Vaalantie 16, Lieto. Tel: (0) 2 487 2898.

Folk music
The semi-official 'capital' of Finnish folk music is the village of **Kaustinen** in Ostrobothnia. Its Folk Music Festival is the largest annual folk music event in the Nordic countries, but Kaustinen is a lively centre for most of the year.

In **Karelia**, look out for performances on the traditional kantele, a stringed instrument best likened to a lyre.

In **Lapland** the *Sámi* tradition is most evident in the distinctive vocal style called *yoik*.

Rock music
Finland has been as much influenced by transatlantic rock and pop as anywhere else. It has some good home-grown rock and folk-rock bands, many of whom make eclectic use of indigenous influences, with electrified kanteles, yoik singing over heavy metal riffs, or just the

HELSINKI THIS WEEK

In Helsinki an excellent source of information about events of all kinds is the free magazine *Helsinki This Week*.
You can read it online at:
www.helsinkiexpert.fi/index_english.html

use of Finnish melodies and cadences. Heavy metal is hugely popular, exemplified by Nightwish and the unlikely Eurovision 2006 winners, Lordi.

HELSINKI
Hartwall Areena

The most likely place to see international stars of rock or other musical genres is Helsinki's largest all-purpose indoor venue, the Hartwall Areena, close to Pasila train station. As well as being home to one of Finland's leading ice-hockey teams, Jokerit, it has recently staged concerts by artists as diverse as Eric Clapton, Iron Maiden, Cirque du Soleil and Snoop Dogg as well as hosting the Eurovision Final in 2007.

Other events held here include Monster Trucks, WWE Wrestling and Disney on Ice. Seating capacity varies according to the event but is around 12,000 at its maximum.
Hartwall Areena, Helsinki Halli Oy, Areenakuja 1, 00240 Helsinki.
Tel: (0) 204 1997;
www.hartwall-areena.com/en

Tavastia Klubi

This is probably the leading venue for rock music in the city.

Urho Kekkosen Katu 4–6, 00100 Helsinki.
Tel: (0) 9 774 67 420;
www.tavastiaklubi.fi

Cinema

Imported films (and TV programmes) are shown in the original language with Finnish subtitles, and new releases normally reach Helsinki at the same time as other European capitals. There are few towns without a cinema.

Nightlife

One of Finland's favourite amusements is the dinner-dance. In smaller places the main hotel of the town is usually the venue, and at weekends people travel from far and wide to join in. The dancing often continues until the small hours. To locate a venue, look for signs saying Tanssiravintola.

Karaoke is also very popular, especially as part of the après-ski scene, and if that's your penchant you won't have a problem finding English-language lyrics to attack.

Helsinki is the key centre for Finnish nightlife, most of it concentrated along the two streets of Uudenmaankatu and Eerikinkatu. They are lined with bars and restaurants, so simply wander along here to find a suitable venue. Many bars stay open till around 3am, clubs typically an hour later.

Theatre

Theatre performances in English are a rarity.

Traditional music thrives in Finland

Children

Finland is safe and child-friendly. When planning a trip, though, especially if you are driving, remember the distances and the sometimes unvarying landscape, and make sure there is enough entertainment for the kids. On railway journeys, some of the trains have play areas for younger children and video facilities for older ones (though the soundtrack will probably be in Finnish).

Many of the outdoor activity providers have special provisions for children. Youngsters would love a visit to a husky farm, which can be found close to nearly all the main centres in the north. The puppies on the farms are an unfailing delight, while a ride on a sled is an attraction for all ages.

Moomin house

Finland is also a perfect place for children to learn to ski. There are plenty of broad, gentle and uncrowded slopes, and the instructors speak good English. All you need to ensure is that they are warmly clothed.

Where to go for kids

The biggest commercial attractions for families with children who go to Finland are Santa Claus Village near Rovaniemi and Moominworld at Naantali (*see pp76–8*). Helsinki has the Linnanmäki Amusement Park and Korkeasaari Zoo (*see pp47–8 and 51*), and another must-see is Moominvalley in Tampere (*see p102*).

Lego Show Helsinki

The Lego Show Helsinki is clearly aimed at youngsters (although it describes itself as 'a theme park for the whole family'). Building and playing with LEGO is the central theme, but there are also bouncy castles, trampolines and other activities. There

Children having fun on snow-shoes at Lake Rautavesi

are specific areas for girls and boys, a café and, naturally, a big LEGO shop. *Sörnäisten rantatie 6, 00530 Helsinki. Tel: (0) 20 710 9902. Open June–Aug daily. Admission charge.*

Turku Castle

Turku Castle has a special programme for children, the Little Knights Tour. Having dressed themselves as Knights of the Cross, children can enjoy a tour of the Castle in the form of a treasure hunt, interspersed with stories of medieval life. At the end, after finding the treasure, participants are dubbed Little Knights of Turku Castle.

Tampere's Särkänniemi Adventure Park

Of its seven attractions, the Dolphinarium and Aquarium of this adventure park would appeal to all ages, while the Planetarium is mainly for older children with a scientific bent of mind. The big attraction for most children is the rides themselves. These include watery rides like the Log River and Rapids Ride, and aerial thrills such as the Corkscrew and Hurricane. Särkänniemi has the largest Half Pipe ride in the world, offering a force of three Gs and speeds of 70kph (43mph). Trombi is said to offer 'the joys and fears of both flight and weightlessness'.

For younger children, there is a special area, Kiddie Land (Ipanaario), with rides like the Piggy Train, Mushroom Race and Rockin' Tug.

Also at Särkänniemi is the Children's Zoo, whose inhabitants include rabbits, puppies, pot-bellied pigs and a family of alpacas.

For additional information, see p103. Tampereen Särkänniemi Ltd, 33230 Tampere. Tel: (0) 207 130 212; www.sarkanniemi.fi

Children

Santa Park

Perhaps the greatest and certainly the most hyped attraction for children in Finland is that it is the home of Santa Claus. While the Santa Claus Village near Rovaniemi has a certain, albeit kitschy, appeal for most ages, the nearby Santa Park is definitely only for youngsters. Santa Claus Village is open every day, but the timings of Santa Park are strictly seasonal. To make the most of it, however, you should visit in winter. It could be hard explaining to the kids why there's no snow 'at the North Pole', but bear in mind that these attractions are very popular, especially in the immediate run-up to Christmas, while if you go too early (the end of November, say), there is a risk of no snow anyway.

To call it a 'park' seems odd as it actually occupies a quarried cavern – or 'magical underground grotto'. Children are encouraged to join Santa's elves in packing presents and making gingerbread, and there are also a number of rides. Santa himself is on hand, too, proving the magical nature of time and space here at the Arctic Circle, since he is also simultaneously present in his office at Santa Claus Village.

96930 Napapiiri, Rovaniemi. Tel: (0) 16 333 0000; www.santapark.com. Closed Mon. Admission charge.

Reindeer Park

There is a Reindeer Park between Santa Claus Village and Santa Park, where you can see and learn about reindeer at

A campfire burns at the Reindeer Park

Finland has many easy-angled slopes suitable for novice skiers

any time of the year. In winter you can take a sleigh ride: in fact, sleigh rides are one way of travelling between the Village and Santa Park.

96930 Napapiiri. www.santaclausvillage. info/reindeerpark/index.htm

In addition, there is a **husky farm** adjacent to Santa Claus Village, and safaris of various lengths are available in winter.

Ranua Zoo

An hour or so from Rovaniemi is Ranua Zoo, which affords a chance to see many of Finland's native wildlife species (and a polar bear) in a more-or-less natural setting. It is a fair walk to get to all the enclosures, but there are games for children along the way. Near the entrance is a small adventure playground and, in summer, a domestic animal zoo, which allows some petting and has donkey or horse rides. The zoo is at its best in winter as many of the animals are much easier to see against the snowy backdrop (this does not apply to the arctic fox, however). The Christmas season (December and early January) is the busiest time. Elves are in attendance and reindeer and snowmobile rides around the grounds are available.

Rovaniementie 29, 97700 Ranua.
Tel: (0) 16 355 1921;
www.ranuazoo.com.
Open daily, summer longer hours.
Admission charge.

Sport and leisure

Outdoor pursuits like hiking, biking, rafting, canoeing, fishing and, in winter, skiing or snowmobiling, are integral to this outdoors-oriented country. Competitive and team sports have an important place too, notably athletics in summer and a range of winter sports – above all ice hockey.

Finland holds a notable place in the history of track and field competition events, having been a member of the Olympic movement even before independence. The most famous Finnish athlete is still Paavo Nurmi, for whom the phrase 'the Flying Finn' was first coined.

Deprived of the opportunity by war in 1916, Nurmi won his first Olympic gold medals in Antwerp in 1920, and achieved his greatest glory in 1924, winning four gold medals in Paris.

Willi Kohlemainen, who won the 5,000 and 10,000m events and the marathon in the 1912 Olympics, is another important national figure. Along with distance running, the Finns have also had a particular affinity for the javelin.

Finland's significance in the world of athletics was recognised in 1952 when Helsinki hosted the Olympic Games (vying with Antwerp as the smallest city ever to do so). More recently, the renovated Olympic Stadium hosted the 2005 World Championships.

Winter sport

Finland's relatively modest fells and lack of high hills have not produced large numbers of ace downhill skiers, and the country is not likely to ever host the Winter Olympics. But the long winters have fostered a great tradition of Nordic events, with many successes in cross-country skiing and ski-jumping, where Matti Nykaenen is one of the greats. Finland has staged many World Cup events in cross-country, ski-jumping and, more recently, freestyle skiing. Most of Finland's ski centres are more suited to beginners and intermediates than advanced skiers. Centres like **Ruka** (*see p140*), **Ylläs** (*see p146*) and **Saariselkä** (*see pp147–9*) are described in the Destination Guide.

Other sports

Finland has also achieved success in a range of other sports, including canoeing and sailing, motor-racing and rallying. The most global of all games, football, is widely played, but is not a

The Finns pursue cross-country skiing in winter

national obsession as it is in Britain. That position is taken by ice-hockey, and, in summer, by Finland's unique version of baseball, pesäpallo, which is played virtually nowhere else.

Golf

Golf has enjoyed growing popularity in Finland as elsewhere, and the country now has more than 60 golf clubs. For a chance to play (almost) under the Midnight Sun, golfers go to Finland's most northerly golf course at Rovaniemi, a few Tiger Woods drives short of the Arctic Circle. It also has a nine-hole ice golf course in winter.

Arctic Golf Finland
Golfkentäntie 1, 96600 Rovaniemi. Tel: (0) 16 345 005.

Even more novel is the course at Tornio, nine holes of which are in Finland and nine in Sweden, and therefore in a different time zone. Even when the sun is below the horizon, at midnight, there is still enough light to play, and therefore you can, given precise timing, hit a drive into the next day or even the next week.

Green Zone Golf Club
Narantie, 95400 Tornio. Tel: (0) 9 698 431711.

ICE HOCKEY

The origins of ice hockey are disputed. Dutch paintings from the 16th century portray a hockey-like game in progress on frozen canals, but the first recorded indoor game took place in Canada in 1875. Inspiration may have come both from European (field) hockey and the Native American lacrosse.

A number of Finnish teams now play in the European league, with even small towns like Rauma and Hämeenlinna, each with populations of around 40,000, supporting highly competitive teams. In 1995 Finland won the World Championship, sparking massive celebrations.

Food and drink

Finnish food had some bad press in 2005, with both the President of France and the Prime Minister of Italy making disparaging comments about it. This is rather unfair however, especially as one can't imagine such dignitaries pop into ordinary restaurants at random. A more balanced judgement would be that in the smaller villages and towns food options may be limited and sometimes uninspired: meals may be filling rather than thrilling.

Larger hotels are usually a reasonable bet for a decent meal, but the low-cost buffet meals are often slightly disappointing – à la carte is dearer but you get what you pay for. Hotel breakfasts, though also buffet-style, are usually much better, with a wide choice. Only rarely, however, will the scrambled eggs be a source of pleasure.

Budget offerings include the inevitable McDonald's and its Finnish equivalent, Hesburger, along with Koti Pizza. A notch or two up the scale is the Rax pizza buffet chain. A very different kind of chain is Fransmanni, associated with Sokos hotels, which offers decent but not particularly cheap meals.

True Finnish cuisine focuses on indigenous produce. Reindeer is a fixture on most menus (smoked reindeer and pineapple pizza, anyone?): it is traditionally sautéed and served with lingonberries and mashed potato. When it's good it's very very good, but in the wrong hands it can remind you of school dinners.

Salmon, both fresh and smoked, is also a regular item on menus. Look out for less familiar fish like vendace and arctic char, or game meat such as the snow grouse.

To eat cheaply while avoiding fast food, head for the *kauppatori* (market square) or *kauppahalli* (market hall); most towns have both. If there isn't a café offering fresh sandwiches you can make your own with delicious Finnish rye bread and a few slices of smoked salmon, reindeer salami or local cheese.

Helsinki is the most cosmopolitan city in Finland. Here, you can get your pick of Vietnamese or Nepalese cuisine, as well as the more usual suspects. It has been claimed that the best Russian food you can get anywhere is to be found in Helsinki.

GOOD-COOKING SYMBOL

For a top-notch Finnish meal, look out for the HelsinkiMenu emblem; it guarantees good cooking with seasonal Finnish ingredients.

FINNISH FOODSTUFFS

leipä	bread
ruisleipä	rye bread
paahtoleipä	toast
tee	tea
omenat	apples
kananmunat	eggs
sokeri	sugar
appelsiini	orange
juusto	cheese
perunat	potatoes
poro	reindeer
kala	fish
lohi	salmon
lakka	cloudberry
olut	beer

Vegetarians

With its chilly climate, Finland is still mainly a land of meat-eaters, but vegetarians are fairly well provided for. The buffet-style hotel breakfasts offer plenty of chance to fill up, while markets will always have a great choice of bread and cheese, and usually fruit as well. There should always be a vegetarian choice in à la carte restaurants, and evening buffets in hotels will give you some sort of an option, even if it is not very inspiring. It is when you are staying in or visiting smaller places, with a set menu, that you need to check in advance. It helps that nearly everyone speaks good English, but be warned that – as in France – it may be assumed that 'vegetarian' means that you eat fish. If you do not, say so. And if you take part in an outdoor excursion that includes a campfire lunch, be aware that nine times out of ten this will be based on sausages.

In the following restaurant listings, the star ratings indicate the average cost of a three-course meal for one excluding alcoholic drinks:

★	less than €15
★★	€15–30
★★★	€30–50
★★★★	over €50

Food and drink

A fabulous setting for coffee and cakes: overlooking Töölönlahti in Helsinki

HELSINKI

Lasipalatsi ★★★

Lasipalatsi means 'Glass Palace' and the restaurant is on the first floor of a recently restored 1930s building with huge windows overlooking the bustle of Mannerheimintie. Traditional Finnish favourites feature on the menu. There is also a ground-floor café.
Mannerheimintie 22–24, 00100 Helsinki. Tel: (0) 20 7424 290.

Ravintola Savoy ★★★★

Dining here is a complete experience, as the interior and all the fittings were designed by Alvar Aalto; its eighth-floor location guarantees great views.
Etelesplanadi 14, 00130 Helsinki.
Tel: (0) 9 684 4020.

Restaurant Havis ★★★★

HelsinkiMenu's 2007 Restaurant of the Year overlooks the harbour and fittingly there's plenty of fresh fish on the menu along with other seasonal ingredients prepared in an imaginative manner.
Eteläranta 16, 00130 Helsinki.
Tel: (0) 9 6869 5660.

Zetor ★★

Huge, centrally located and immensely popular, Zetor is the sort of place you either love or hate. However, its tractor-themed décor and self-conscious wackiness shouldn't obscure the fact that it offers a wide range of reasonably priced food and great choice of beers.
Kaivopiha, Mannerheimintie 3–5, 00100 Helsinki.
Tel: (0) 9 666 966.

SOUTHWEST FINLAND AND THE WEST COAST

Turku

Herman ★★★★

Yet another brewery-restaurant, but definitely oriented towards fine dining, Herman is found in an old waterfront building near the Föri. Top-quality fresh dishes and fine wines as well as great beer. The set Turku Menu is an economical choice.
Läntinen Rantakatu 3, 20100 Turku.
Tel: (0) 2 230 3333.

Old Bank ★★

Turku specialises in pub-restaurants in unusual surroundings. Possibly the best known is the

Helsinki's mobile pub-tram is an unusual setting for a drink (*see p50*)

Old Bank (the English name is used), offering over 150 varieties of beer and decent food too.
Aurakatu 3, 20100 Turku.
Tel: (0) 2 274 5700.

Panimoravintola Koulu ★★★

A more conventional place, *Panimo* means brewery and indeed it brews several fine beers in various styles. It is housed in a grand neo-classical building, too. Downstairs is a pleasant pub, and upstairs a smart

---

FINNISH BEER

Beer – *olut* in Finnish – is one of the main lubricants of life. It is quite normal, for instance, to take a few bottles into the sauna. The 13th of October is national beer day. Most of the output of major brewers like Koff, Karhu and Lapin Kulta is lager, but there are many breweries where dark beers, ales and porters can all be found. The traditional *sahti* is one of the oldest beers still brewed anywhere in the world.

The Finnish Society for Traditional Beers, Perinteisen Oluen Seura, has English pages on its website: *www.posbeer.org*

à la carte restaurant.
Eerikinkatu 18, 20100 Turku.
Tel: (0) 2 274 5757.

Uusi Apteekki

Koulu supplies beer to Uusi Apteekki (New Apothecary), a pure pub (no food) in the unusual setting of a former pharmacy, with many of the original furnishings and fittings retained.
Kaskenkatu 1, 20700 Turku.
Tel: (0) 2250 2595.

Naantali
Kala-Trappi ★★★★

In nearby Naantali, Kala-Trappi is a gourmet restaurant with a nautical theme to its décor. The rooms at the back are cosy, those at the front enjoy an expansive view over the harbour.
Nunnakatu 3.
Tel: (0) 2 435 2477;
www.kalatrappi.fi

Tampere

Tampere makes a fair amount of fuss about its culinary speciality, *mustamakkara*, sometimes described as 'blood sausage', but any

Lancastrian will realise right away that it's a black pudding, and often not a bad one.

The city has plenty of good restaurants, with a broad selection close together in the Finlayson complex.

Panimoravintola Plevna ★★

One of the most popular restaurants, it brews some fine beers and cider. On the menu, sausages are a definite speciality, but there are also fish dishes and vegetarian options.
Itäinenkatu 8 (Finlayson area).
Tel: (0) 3 2601 200.

Ravintola Näsinneula ★★★★

There is no question that the best view in Tampere is from Ravintola Näsinneula, atop the observation tower of the same name. The food is top-quality and, as the restaurant revolves, you can watch the view change as you dine.
Särkänniemi, Tampere.
Tel: (0) 3 2488 234.

Hotels and accommodation

As with shopping, accommodation in Finland is not cheap, and the standards are generally high. Again, the rates are broadly comparable to Britain, or at least Britain outside London. There is a premium on hotels in central Helsinki but those are not exorbitant in the way London notoriously is.

Finland offers every type of accommodation you can think of, from spartan wilderness shelters to luxury hotels. There are several chains which offer accommodation of a similar standard in most of their hotels, typically catering for business travellers and tourists. Finnish holidaymakers tend to flock to camping grounds and holiday villages, where hotel rates are low in summer. In ski centres, there is a substantial premium to be paid in the winter months.

The largest chain is the Sokos group, with 37 hotels in 26 cities plus one in Tallinn. Others are Cumulus, Finlandia and Scandic: all are generally reliable, though the hotels can be bland.

It is also worth knowing about the Finncheque system, recognised in more than 140 hotels across the country, which is both an economical and convenient way to cover the cost of accommodation.

Prices start at €37 B&B per person in the cheaper Category II hotels (2007 rate). By purchasing the 'cheques' in advance you secure a reasonable discount on the standard rate.
More details at
www.visitfinland.com/ web/finncheque/index.nsf

It would be a surprise to find any member of the hotel staff who does not speak at least basic English.

In the following listings, the star ratings indicate the average cost of accommodation for a single room including breakfast:

★   less than €25
★★   €25–40
★★★   €40–60
★★★★   over €60

Hotels
HELSINKI
Hotel Helka ★★★
This former YWCA building has been completely revamped to create a smart hotel, close to Temppeliaukio and the Tennis Palace and within walking distance of the city centre. Rooms are

compact but chic, with crafty use of space and stylish features.
Pohjoinen Rautatiekatu 23 A, 00100 Helsinki.
Tel: (0) 9 613 580;
www.helka.fi

Hotel Kämp ★★★★
Without doubt, this is the most famous hotel in the city. Since 1887 it has had a central place in Finnish history, from being the venue for meetings of members of the independence movement to being the base for war correspondents from 1940–45. Recently restored, it is an elegant as well as central place to stay.
Pohjoisesplanadi 29, 00100 Helsinki.
Tel: (0) 9 576 111;
www.hotelkamp.fi/en

Scandic Hotel Simonkenttä ★★★★
Picking a hotel in central Helsinki is somewhat invidious as one is naturally spoilt for choice, but Scandic Hotel Simonkenttä has a good location, comfortable rooms and an award-

winning chef.
Simonkatu 9, 00100 Helsinki.
Tel: (0) 968 380;
www.scandic-hotels.com

HELSINKI ENVIRONS
Porvoo
Haikko Manor Spa Hotel ★★★★
A few kilometres from Porvoo, this hotel gives you two for the price of one. The main hotel is a modern, standard establishment with a spa on the premises. The adjacent Manor House, however, is rather special, a classical manor, furnished with antiques and heated with green energy from the sea.
Haikkontie 114, 06400 Porvoo.
Tel: (0) 19 576 01;
www.haikko.fi

SOUTHWEST FINLAND AND THE WEST COAST
Turku
Best Western Turku Hotel Seaport ★★★
Its location just a stone's throw from the ferries makes this a perfect choice for anyone arriving late or leaving

early to/from Åland or Sweden. It's also very close to Turku Castle and there are excellent bus connections to the city centre. The hotel has been pleasantly converted from an old customs shed and most rooms give a view of the comings and goings at the port.
Matkustajasatama, 20100 Turku. Tel: (0) 2 283 3000; www.hotelseaport.fi

Turku Hotel Centro ★★★
Centro has a great location, in the city centre but tucked away in a quiet courtyard. Rooms are small but designer-stylish without sacrificing comfort, and there's free wireless internet access.
Yliopistonkatu 12a, 20100 Turku.
Tel: (0) 2 469 0469.

Naantali
Naantali Spa Hotel ★★★★
Naantali Spa Hotel may not be the 'best' hotel in Finland, but it certainly ranks among the most luxurious. Alongside is the Sunborn Princess floating hotel.

*Matkailijantie 2, 21100
Naantali.
Tel: (0) 2 445 5800;
www.naantalispa.fi/
english/index.html*

SOUTHEAST FINLAND AND THE LAKE DISTRICT

Åland Islands

Hotel Arkipelag ★★★★

Probably Mariehamn's top-rated hotel, Arkipelag overlooks the guest marina in the East Harbour.
*Strandgatan 31, 22100
Mariehamn.
Tel: (0) 18 24 020;
www.hotellarkipelag.com*

Savonlinna

Hotel Seurahuone ★★★

The hotel has a spot-on location right by the passenger quay and marketplace in Savonlinna, and all the rooms have lake views.
*Kauppatori 4–6, 57130
Savonlinna.
Tel: (0) 15 7395 500;
www.savonhotelli.fi*

Tampere

Hotel Tammer ★★★★

All the usual hotel chains are represented in the centre of Tampere, but one of the Sokos offerings stands out. Hotel Tammer – sometimes prefixed with 'Grand' – is one of the more venerable hotels of Finland, and has an unbeatable location overlooking the Tammerkoski rapids.
*Sokos Hotel Tammer,
Satakunnankatu 13,
33100 Tampere.
Tel: (0) 20 1234 632.*

Jyväskylä

Boutique Hotel Yöpuu ★★★★

An elegant 19th-century building with 26 rooms, each individually furnished and decorated.
*Yliopistonkatu 23, 40100
Jyväskylä.
Tel: (0) 14 333 900;
www.hotelliyopuu.fi*

Pori

Yyteri Spa Hotel (Yyterin Kylpylähotelli) ★★★

The hotel might win no prizes for beauty, at least from the outside, but plenty for location. It is just metres from what is probably the best beach in Finland, and every room has a sea view.
*Sipintie 1, 28840 Pori.
Tel: (0) 2 628 5300.*

NORTH FINLAND

Ivalo

Hotel Ivalo ★★★

Hotel Ivalo makes an excellent base to explore northern Lapland.
*Ivalontie 34, 99800 Ivalo.
Tel: (0) 16 688 111;
www.hotelivalo.fi*

Rovaniemi

Hotel Santa Claus ★★

There just had to be a Hotel Santa Claus in Rovaniemi. But there is no need to be embarrassed, as it is actually a fine place to stay with very comfortable rooms.
*Clarion Hotel Santa
Claus, Korkalonkatu 29,
96200 Rovaniemi.
Tel: (0) 16 321 321;
www.hotelsantaclaus.fi*

Bed and breakfast

The 'B&B' abbreviation is universally recognised in Finland (in Finnish it would be S&A). Bed and Breakfast, especially in rural areas, typically offers comfortable accommodation and a personal welcome that's missing in the big hotels. En-suite facilities are not guaranteed, however.

Standards are high and rates compare favourably with similar B&Bs in the UK. Local tourist offices, brochures and websites will always be able to recommend one. Don't, however, rely on B&Bs being open for business if you turn up outside the summer season.

Cottages and cabins

There's a real Finnish flavour to staying in a cabin in the woods. Many Finnish families have their own '*mokki*' or cottage and these are often quite basic, but those marketed to foreign visitors will have all the modern amenities. They are often in quite remote locations so you need to be fairly self-sufficient, though larger complexes will have a restaurant and perhaps a small shop on site. It is a lot more convenient to stay in a cabin if you have a car, though you can get just about anywhere by a combination of train, bus and taxi.

Prices peak in summer and winter, when you will normally need to book on a weekly basis. In the low season, cabins are likely to be available for a weekend stay. A number of companies offer booking services.

Lomarengas – Finnish Country Holidays (rates vary)

Claims the 'widest selection of cottages to rent in Finland', around 1,300 of them.
Lomarengas – Finnish Country Holidays Ltd, Etelüesplanadı 22 C, 00130 Helsinki.
Tel: (0) 9 5766 3350;
www.lomarengas.fi

FinnishLakeside Cabins.com (rates vary)

They have a smaller selection, around 200 cottages and cabins, but are UK-based and targeted specifically at British visitors.
FinnishLakesideCabins. com, 2 Dairy Lodges, Hatfield Park, Hatfield, Hertfordshire, AL9 5NH, Tel: (0) 170 725 6398;
www. finnishlakesidecabins.com

Hotel Kakslauttanen
★★★

Hotel Kakslauttanen, about 10km (6 miles) south of Saariselkä, is not really a hotel at all, but a collection of cabins with a central restaurant. In summer the choice is limited to the log cabins among the trees, but in winter there is also Finland's first igloo village. There are permanent glass igloos where you can lie in bed under the Northern Lights, and every winter genuine snow igloos are built.
99830 Saariselkä.
Tel: (0) 16 667 100;
www.kakslauttanen.fi

Karelian Village (rates vary)

There's a little bit of everything at Bomba, near Nurmes, in Karelia: simple but comfortable cabins in the 'Karelian village', self-catering cottages, and a hotel with attached spa.
Suojärvenkatu 1, 75500 Nurmes.
Tel: (0) 13 687 200;
www.bomba.fi

Practical guide

Arriving

By air

Flying is the most convenient way to reach Finland from most countries, and nearly all international flights arrive in Helsinki. There are direct flights from most European countries and from several North American cities. As Helsinki is the closest European city by the Great Circle route to East Asia, Finnair also specialises in routes to the Far East, with direct services to several Chinese cities, Tokyo, Bangkok and Singapore, which are also advantageous to travellers from Australia and New Zealand.

The airport at Vantaa has regular buses to Helsinki's city centre. A rapid rail link is under construction.

By rail

Getting to Finland by train is long-winded, unless you happen to be coming from Russia. Direct daily trains from St Petersburg to Helsinki take about six hours (a high-speed service is planned). The only other rail link is through northern Sweden, and even this requires a short bus transfer. Unless your destination is Lapland anyway, those who don't want to fly are better advised to take a train to Stockholm and then a ferry to Turku or Helsinki.

By road

As with the rail, driving to Finland is very long-winded. There are road crossings to Sweden and Norway, but these are in the far north and can only be recommended as part of a grand tour taking in one or both of these countries as well. It is generally much easier to bring a car via one of the ferry services noted below. It is easier still, and usually cheaper, to hire a car on arrival.

By sea

There are regular car-ferry services to/from several European ports, principally Stockholm. Some of these are among the largest ferries in the world, resembling cruise liners. Viking Line and Silja Line both run daily

A traditional wooden boat at the Nauvo Islands

services between Helsinki and Stockholm, which take about 16 hours. Stockholm to Turku is shorter, about 11 hours. However, the shortest crossing from Sweden to Finland is further north, from Umea to Vaasa – a mere three hours.

In addition, there are services from Rostock in Germany, to Helsinki and to the port of Hanko, Finland's southernmost town.

The shortest sea crossing to Finland is from Tallinn in Estonia.

Entry formalities

Visitors from EU countries may enter Finland without a passport if they have a valid national identity card. As Britain does not yet issue such cards, British citizens still require a passport. Citizens of many other countries, including Australia, Canada, New Zealand and the USA, may enter without visas.

All foreign nationals other than citizens of the Nordic countries must obtain a residence permit if planning to stay for more than three months.

Camping

The outdoors-loving Finns are keen campers and there are more than 200 recognised sites around the country, though many are open only in the summer months. Camper vans are popular, rather than huge American-style RVs, which are too big for parking in most sites. Tents are nearly always available.

Under 'Every Man's Right' there is wide scope for 'wild' camping, which is obviously free.

If you are on a camping trip outside the summer season, you will need a good insulating mat and sleeping bag. In summer mosquito netting and/or repellant are essential.

Climate

Finland's climate is more benign than many people expect. Summers in the south are quite warm, with temperatures comparable to Britain but with less rain and longer hours of daylight (there is no real darkness at midsummer). In the north it is cooler but still usually pleasant, and the sun shines round the clock.

Winter is much colder than in Britain, with temperatures in Helsinki consistently below freezing point for three months or more. The further north you go, the longer and colder the winters are: in Lapland daytime temperatures may stay below −10°C (14°F) for months, and often hover around −20°C (−4°F). However, the cold is less forbidding than most people (certainly Britons) expect, as it is usually dry and not too windy. Warm clothing is necessary, of course, but those who are planning active recreation are often in danger of piling on too many layers and overheating.

Autumn is a popular time for hiking: the days are cool and crisp, although by the end of September temperatures can easily drop below freezing point at night.

Practical guide

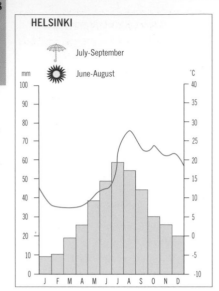

HELSINKI

July–September

June–August

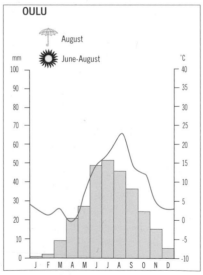

OULU

August

June–August

WEATHER CONVERSION CHART

25.4mm = 1 inch
°F = 1.8 × °C + 32

Crime

Finland generally has a low crime rate compared to the US and most other European countries, and visitors are unlikely to find themselves victims of crime. In the rural areas it is still quite common for cars and homes to be left unlocked. It is also the case that there are no real large-scale 'don't-go areas' like those in the US and some European cities. Street crimes like mugging and theft are uncommon, but not unheard of. Although the risk is low, it still makes sense to take the normal precautions.

Finns are heavy drinkers and this can result in a degree of rowdiness, but usually remains relatively good-humoured: the 'yob culture' and binge drinking that disfigure many British towns and cities are little in evidence. Alcohol abuse, coupled with isolation and the long dark nights of winter, contribute to a relatively high suicide rate and to domestic violence, but these are unlikely to impinge on the visitor.

Customs regulations

Finland is a member of the EU, and there are no restrictions on imports from other EU countries, except alcohol and tobacco. The limits for these are:
Alcohol (18 years or older)
3 litres of aperitif (maximum 22%) or sparkling wine, 5 litres of other wines, 64 litres of beer.
If you are 20 years or older the limit is the above plus 1 litre of spirits.
Tobacco (17 years or older)

300 cigarettes OR 150 cigarillos (maximum 3g each) OR 75 cigars OR 400g (14oz) pipe tobacco/loose cigarette tobacco.

The limits for travellers arriving from outside the EU are:

Alcohol (18 years or older)

2 litres of aperitif (maximum 22%) or sparkling wine AND 2 litres of other wines, 16 litres of beer.

If you are 20 years or older the limit is the above plus 1 litre of spirits.

Tobacco (17 years or older)

200 cigarettes OR 100 cigarillos (maximum 3g each) OR 50 cigars OR 250g (9oz) pipe tobacco/loose cigarette tobacco.

Driving

In most respects driving in Finland is easy. The traffic is light (outside city centres) and drivers are generally polite. Yet some qualification is needed.

In the main cities there is little need for a car to get around and in Helsinki it

MIDGES AND MOSQUITOES

Finland's short and intense summers encourage not just a rapid flowering of plant life, but an equally rapid and dramatic growth of midges and mosquitoes. These are particularly prevalent in the north, and near swamps and still water, but be prepared to encounter them anywhere between May and August. If you don't have a repellant, ask for one at any pharmacy (*apteekki*), where a range of both chemical and natural products will be available. In wilderness areas many people, especially hunters and anglers, wear fine-mesh head coverings.

CONVERSION TABLE

FROM	TO	MULTIPLY BY
Inches	Centimetres	2.54
Feet	Metres	0.3048
Yards	Metres	0.9144
Miles	Kilometres	1.6090
Acres	Hectares	0.4047
Gallons	Litres	4.5460
Ounces	Grams	28.35
Pounds	Grams	453.6
Pounds	Kilograms	0.4536
Tons	Tonnes	1.0160

To convert back, for example from centimetres to inches, divide by the number in the third column.

MEN'S SUITS

UK	36	38	40	42	44	46	48
Rest of Europe	46	48	50	52	54	56	58
USA	36	38	40	42	44	46	48

DRESS SIZES

UK	8	10	12	14	16	18
France	36	38	40	42	44	46
Italy	38	40	42	44	46	48
Rest of Europe	34	36	38	40	42	44
USA	6	8	10	12	14	16

MEN'S SHIRTS

UK	14	14.5	15	15.5	16	16.5	17
Rest of Europe	36	37	38	39/40	41	42	43
USA	14	14.5	15	15.5	16	16.5	17

MEN'S SHOES

UK	7	7.5	8.5	9.5	10.5	11
Rest of Europe	41	42	43	44	45	46
USA	8	8.5	9.5	10.5	11.5	12

WOMEN'S SHOES

UK	4.5	5	5.5	6	6.5	7
Rest of Europe	38	38	39	39	40	41
USA	6	6.5	7	7.5	8	8.5

is a positive hindrance, especially when it comes to parking. Trams, buses and cycles are quicker and more convenient. Elsewhere, driving and parking are easy but it should be borne in mind that distances can be long and that many of the roads are monotonous. There are few motorways, none north of Tampere, so speeds are not particularly high. Losing concentration, even falling asleep at the wheel, are real hazards.

Nevertheless, in many areas, especially in Lapland, the convenience of a car is hard to deny; public transport will get you almost anywhere but it can be slow. A good compromise may be to bridge long distances by air or train and to hire a car for travel within a region. Another option that is worth considering is shipping a car by

Relaxed driving on the Åland Islands

train. Night trains with car-carriers link Helsinki and Tampere to Oulu, Kolari and Rovaniemi; there is also a service from Turku to Kolari. Sleeping through the journey means no time is wasted, and considering that a night's accommodation is included it also works out to be remarkably economical.

In general, driving rules are straightforward: drive on the right and overtake from the left. As a rule, traffic on the right has priority, but main highways (indicated by a yellow diamond) are priority roads, as are motorways. Standard **speed limits** are 50kph (31mph) in built-up areas and 80kph (50mph) elsewhere, but many highways through open country or forest have a 100kph (62mph) limit. Use dipped headlights at all times; in a hired car they will come on automatically. Seat belts are compulsory.

Throughout the country many of the minor roads are unsurfaced and require careful driving. You may see Finns driving amazingly fast on these, but it takes practice (this is one reason why Finland has produced many winning rally drivers). In winter you will need special tyres, and lower speed limits apply on some of the roads.

Driving under the influence of alcohol is illegal, and the Finnish police are at their most visible when carrying out random checks, not just on Saturday nights but Sunday mornings too.

One road hazard that you won't meet in Britain is that of wandering reindeer and elk. Reindeer will be encountered only in the northern half of the country but they are common there: they are most likely to be a hazard in summer when irritated by insects. Elk are less common but can be encountered almost anywhere, and a collision with a 400kg (63-stone) elk is definitely to be avoided.

The main **emergency number** is **112**. **Accidents** should also be reported as soon as possible to the Finnish Motor Insurers' Centre, Green Card Bureau and Guarantee Fund (Liikennevakuut-uskeskus) (*Bulevardi 28, 00120 Helsinki; tel: (0) 9 680 401*).

Finland belongs to the 'green card' system, which includes the UK and Ireland. Drivers bringing cars from these countries must have valid **insurance**; they are not required to carry the green card itself, but it is recommended. Vehicles from other countries need to obtain 'frontier insurance' on entry.

The cost of **petrol** is higher than in most European countries, approaching that in Britain, and the distances covered tend to be greater than in Britain. Leaded petrol is not available. **Diesel** is substantially cheaper than petrol. Filling stations, usually with a restaurant on the premises, are reasonably frequent on the main highways in the south but are far apart in Lapland. Many filling stations have automated pumps, available 24 hours, where you can pay by cash or card (but usually only cards issued in Finland). There is usually a touch-screen system and the menu is often available in English.

Car hire
This is relatively expensive compared to America or some other European countries, but not too far above British rates. Availability is widespread, with hire offices at airports and main railway stations as well as town centres. Opening hours can be limited, so it is advisable to check ahead. To hire a car all you need is a valid driving licence.

Electricity
The electricity supply is 220V, 50Hz AC and the plugs are the standard two-pin type found across much of northern Europe. Visitors from Britain will need a plug adaptor but the voltage is compatible.

Embassies
Canada *Pohjoisesplanadi 25 B, 00101 Helsinki. Tel: (0) 9 228 530.*
UK *Itäinen Puistotie 17, 00140 Helsinki. Tel: (0) 9 2286 5100.*
USA *Itäinen Puistotie 14 B, 00140 Helsinki. Tel: (0) 9 616 250.*

Australian and NZ citizens contact:
The Australian Consulate *C/Tradimex Oy, Museokatu 25 B, 00100 Helsinki. Tel: (0) 9 4777 6640.*
Finnish embassies in other countries:
Australia *12 Darwin Avenue, Yarralumla, ACT 2600. Tel: (61) 2 6273 3800.*

Canada *850–855 Metcalfe St., Ottawa, ON K1P 6L5. Tel: (001) 236 2389.*
United Kingdom *8 Chesham Place, London, SW1X 8HW. Tel: (44) 20 7838 6200.*
United States Embassy in Washington, Consulates in New York and Los Angeles. Refer to *www.finland.org/en/* to be directed to the appropriate one, or *tel: (001) 298 5800.*

Emergency telephone numbers
The normal emergency number is **112**.

Health
Finland has few health hazards, but travel insurance is always advisable. The public health system is good and EU citizens are entitled to access it: British visitors are advised to carry the European Health Insurance card, available from any UK post office. Pharmacies (*Apteekki*) offer good advice and a wide range of remedies, and are often open into the evening. Tap water is safe to drink, but lakes and streams are, sadly, often polluted. Even in the wilderness there may be a paper plant somewhere upstream, or a dead reindeer, and purification tablets or filters should be carried if you need to drink from streams.

Insurance
Although Finland is a safe country, it is a good idea to have valid travel insurance. There are unlikely to be any special restrictions or higher premiums, unless you plan engaging in 'hazardous' activities like downhill skiing.

Internet access
Internet access is widely available, notably in public libraries. There are fewer internet cafés than in some other countries. Upmarket hotels often have access, including Wi-Fi, which is also available in major airports.

Maps
Genimap (Finnish Survey) is the official body equivalent to Britain's Ordnance Survey, and produces a range of maps of similarly high quality. For a broad view of a region, and not only if you're driving, the most useful series is the Karttakeskus 200K Road Maps of Finland at a scale of 1:200,000. This is now being replaced by a new series at scale 1:250,000. These maps show topographic detail and a range of tourist information, and there is an English key to the symbols used.

For walking, cycling and other outdoor pursuits, the 1:50,000 series is excellent. In addition to all the information you'd expect on a British OS map, there is less familiar detail indicating, for instance, cross-country ski tracks and snowmobile routes. It takes just a little practice to distinguish between the various categories: hiking routes usually skirt round lakes and swamps, while ski and snowmobile routes often go straight across.

Local tourist offices will have free or cheap maps of the locality.

Practical guide

Media

There are no English-language newspapers in Finland other than tourist-oriented information sheets. British and American papers (notably the *International Herald Tribune*) are available, at a price, at R-kiosks and major rail stations.

However, you will not be short of reading material; as many books are not translated into Finnish, Finns tend to read them in English and bookshops normally have an English section. There is an English-language news summary daily at 10.55pm on the national radio stations YLE3 and YLE4. Capital FM, a Helsinki station, relays programmes from English-language stations.

The main TV networks show British and American films and series, with Finnish subtitles. Hotels often have CNN, Sky News, BBC World, etc.

Money matters

The currency in Finland is the euro. There are no restrictions on the import or export of currency. All the main international credit cards are widely accepted and ATMs (*Otto*) are widespread.

Opening hours

Opening hours of shops and other establishments do vary, and what many visitors to Finland notice is the number of shops, restaurants and tourist attractions that are open only in the summer months.

Typical hours are 9am–6pm or later on weekdays. Saturday closing is often earlier. Sunday opening is patchy, and larger stores are limited by law. For these, Sunday opening is permitted only from June to August and in December. Smaller stores may remain open from noon–9pm. Banks are normally open Monday–Friday 9am–4pm and closed on weekends.

Police

The Finnish police (*Poliis*) are relatively few in number, a testament to the generally low levels of crime, and the average visitor will never need to interact with them. Often they are only seen when conducting random breath or speed checks on the roads. Nevertheless, every town has a police station.

Trams share the streets with cars in Helsinki

Language

Finnish is an unusual language. Apart from Sámi and Estonian, and a more distant kinship with Hungarian, it bears almost no relation to other European languages. The Finns are well aware of this and, though fiercely proud of their language, they do not expect visitors to master its complexities.

Fortunately for the visitor, English is universally taught in schools and most Finns speak it at least passably and often very well. Very few, mostly older, people speak no English at all. You'll also frequently find English translations alongside Finnish and Swedish in everything from restaurant menus to the notice that tells you not to lean out of the window on the train.

Large bookshops carry an extensive selection of titles in English, not for the benefit of visitors or expatriates, but for the locals. With only five million Finnish speakers, much of world literature either never appears in translation or does so only after a considerable wait, and many Finns read the latest bestsellers in English.

It should not be forgotten that Finland is a bilingual country. Every street name in Helsinki, for instance, comes in two versions, so that Aleksanderinkatu is also Alexandergatn. This bilingualism occasionally comes in handy. If you are trying to puzzle out a sign or notice, the English speaker stands almost no chance of making sense of the Finnish, but Swedish is from the same linguistic family as English and sometimes you can make an educated guess at to what it means.

The one exception to the bilingual rule is in the Åland Islands, where Swedish is the sole official language, but here, too, English is almost universally spoken. In the far north, the Sámi language (related to Finnish) also appears, sometimes in preference to Swedish, on official publications and signs.

Apart from English, the other foreign languages that are most widely spoken are, not surprisingly, Russian and German.

Of course, it's always a good idea to pick up at least a few basic words and phrases. People do appreciate any effort that you make and will invariably be tolerant if you mangle the language – though they may politely correct you. Note that the stress falls on the first syllable; English speakers will often tend to stress the second syllable, which is one way that Finns can easily identify us!

BASIC PHRASES

good morning	hyvaa huomenta
good evening	hyvaa iltaa
goodbye	nakemiin
yes	kyllä
no	ei
excuse me	anteeksi

SIGNS AND PLACES

entrance	sisään
exit	ulos
open	avoinna
closed	suljettu
information	opastus (but info and the i symbol widely used)
station	asema
railway station	rautatieasema
bus station	linja-autoasema
airport	lentoasema
café	kahvila or café
restaurant	ravintola
bar	baari

DAYS OF THE WEEK

Monday	Maantanai
Tuesday	Tiistai
Wednesday	Keskiviikko
Thursday	Torstai
Friday	Perjantai
Saturday	Lauantai
Sunday	Sunnuntai

NUMBERS

1	yksi
2	kaksi
3	kolme
4	neljä
5	viisi
6	kuusi
7	seitsemän
8	kahdeksan
9	yhdeksän
10	kymmenen

Post offices

Post offices are open Monday–Friday 9am–6pm and are closed on weekends.

Public holidays

The two main public holidays are Christmas and Midsummer (the weekend after the solstice), when almost everything, including tourist attractions, shuts down. In fact, most places tend to close at midday on Midsummer Eve and Christmas Eve. In Karelia, where the Orthodox tradition is strong, Easter is celebrated with greater enthusiasm even than Christmas. On other public holidays most shops and all banks are closed, but other attractions may remain open. The national holidays are:

1 January New Year's Day
6 January Epiphany
March/April variable Easter
1 May May Day
40 days after Easter Ascension Day
Variable Midsummer's Day
1 November All Saints' Day
6 December Independence Day
25 December Christmas

Public transport

Finland has an excellent public transport network, and there are few places beyond its reach.

The railway system is state-run and has been so ever since its inception. Finland has one of the highest figures in Europe for kilometres of track per head of population. Trains between the main centres, especially on the Helsinki–Turku–Tampere triangle, are fast and frequent. Pride of place goes to the Pendolino fleet, but anyone used to the relatively cramped British Pendolino trains is in for a pleasant surprise.

In fact, all Finnish trains will strike British visitors as unusually spacious. This is partly due to the fact that

Trains run despite the snow

Local ferries link the principal islands

Finland, in common with Russia, uses a broader gauge of track, 1,524mm or 5ft, as compared to the 1,435mm or 4ft 8½in more common in the rest of Europe and North America. The 'loading gauge' (space allowed for platforms, bridges, etc.) is also generous and allows comfortable double-decker trains to be used.

Ticket prices are based on distance and on the class of train you are travelling on: after the Pendolino comes the InterCity, which is also comfortable and reasonably speedy.

For those travelling to the north, an excellent way to get there is by sleeper train. Overnight trains link Helsinki via Tampere to destinations such as Oulu, Rovaniemi and Kemijarvi. Since the train also serves as a night's accommodation, no time is wasted and it works out cheaper than flying. And there is something undeniably romantic about going to bed in an urban setting

and waking up the next morning to a view of endless lakes and forests.

For details and timetables of trains and ferries in Finland consult the *Thomas Cook European Timetable*, which is available to buy online at www.thomascookpublishing.com, from Thomas Cook branches in the UK or by calling 01733 416477. The Finnish Railways website *www.vr.fi/heo/eng/index.html* is also extremely useful.

Internal flights, most of which are operated by Finnair, are of course the quickest way to get from point A to B, and to reach destinations like Inari in the far north beyond the limits of the rail network. However, two drawbacks must be noted: these flights are relatively expensive, and while all regional airports have regular flights to Helsinki, there are fewer links between them. It is not possible to fly directly from Inari to Rovaniemi, for instance.

For journeys like that, and many others not covered by air or rail, there is (almost) always a bus. ExpressBus services run just about everywhere: any town or village large enough to have a post office is probably on the network. Distances are long, especially in the north, and the roads are not particularly fast, so journey times can be lengthy. On the other hand, the buses are cheap and pretty comfortable. There may well be an onboard toilet (and it will be clean), and, if not, the driver will stop every couple of hours at a service station.

It is worth knowing that long-distance buses will carry bikes, provided there is space in the luggage compartment.

All towns have local bus services. Fares are often at a flat rate and can be relatively high for shorter journeys. Day passes or multi-trip tickets are cheaper: these can be bought from the driver or an R-kiosk. Helsinki has trams and a metro, with a shared ticketing system. The Helsinki Card gives you free travel on public transport as well as free or discounted admission to museums, etc. Turku and Tampere have similar cards.

Sustainable tourism

Thomas Cook is a strong advocate of ethical and fairly traded tourism and believes that the travel experience should be as good for the places visited as it is for the people that visit them. That's why we're a firm supporter of The Travel Foundation, a charity that develops solutions to help improve and protect holiday destinations, their environment, traditions and culture. To find out what you can do to make a positive difference to the places you travel to and the people who live there, please visit
www.thetravelfoundation.org.uk

Telephones

Local and international calls can be made from phone booths, hotels and sometimes post offices. Public phones usually require a card for payment: these are obtainable from R-kiosks and some post offices.

Finland has near-comprehensive network coverage for mobile phone users: only in the remote wilderness is there likely to be no signal.

The country code for phoning from abroad to Finland is **358**; then omit the first 0 in the Finnish area code. To make an international call from inside Finland dial 00 followed by the country code, for example:
UK 00 44
USA and Canada 00 1

Time

Finland is two hours ahead of Britain and one hour ahead of most of Europe.

Tipping

In general, tipping is not expected in Finland. An exception may be made for service and in upmarket restaurants. Taxi drivers are happy to 'keep the change'.

Toilets

Toilets are always clean. However, public toilets are relatively rare and almost never free. It is worth retaining a supply of 50 cent and 1 euro coins. The best places to look for free toilets are large department stores, museums and libraries. Those at train and bus stations will charge, often a euro or more. Bars and restaurants may also charge you for using their facilities.

Tourist information

Finnish municipalities invariably recognise the importance of tourism and are willing to invest in promoting and facilitating it. The result is that virtually anywhere you go you will find a tourist information centre, often new and highly sophisticated. The staff will usually speak at least a modicum of English and there is a good chance that literature in English will be available too. If you wish to research your destination before you go, it is almost certain to have a website and that website in turn is almost certain to have at least its most relevant pages in English.

The Finnish Tourist Board has offices in many countries and its website is an excellent starting point. When in Finland, you can phone its main office. *PO Box 625, Töölönkatu 11, 00101 Helsinki.*
Tel: (0) 10 6058 000;
www.visitfinland.com;
email: mek@mek.fi

Travellers with disabilities

Finland is reasonably well equipped for travellers with disabilities. Wheelchair access to museums, galleries, shops and hotels is required by law. Local buses are normally wheelchair-friendly. Boarding a train may require assistance as the platforms are low and the older carriages have high steps, but a ramp or hoist will be available. The newer InterCity and Pendolino trains have easy access, though there is no easy way to get to the upper deck on the InterCity trains.

The Finnish organisation for travellers with disabilities is Rullaten Ry. Its website has very little in English, but there is a contact form. *Pajutie 7, 02770 Espoo.*
Tel: (0) 9 805 7393; www.rullaten.fi

Checking the route (local area maps are usually available free)

Index

Acknowledgements

Thomas Cook Publishing wishes to thank Jon Sparks for the photographs in this book, to whom the copyright belongs, except for the following images:

FINNISH TOURIST BOARD 29, 32
FLICKR/Peruvuoj 33, Sami Keinänen 54, 62, Uninen 90, Tuija 110, 111
THOMAS COOK PUBLISHING 1, 27, 138, 145, 164
WIKIMEDIA COMMONS/Anon 16, 39, Vladimir Menkov 19, Thermos 23
WORLD PICTURES/PHOTOSHOT 163

For CAMBRIDGE PUBLISHING MANAGEMENT LTD:
Maps: PCGraphics (UK) LTD
Project editor: ROSALIND MUNRO
Proofreader: JAN McCANN
Typesetter: TREVOR DOUBLE

SEND YOUR THOUGHTS TO
BOOKS@THOMASCOOK.COM

We're committed to providing the very best up-to-date information in our travel guides and constantly strive to make them as useful as they can be. You can help us to improve future editions by letting us have your feedback. If you've made a wonderful discovery on your travels that we don't already feature, if you'd like to inform us about recent changes to anything that we do include, or if you simply want to let us know your thoughts about this guidebook and how we can make it even better – we'd love to hear from you.

Send us ideas, discoveries and recommendations today and then look out for your valuable input in the next edition of this title.

Emails to the above address, or letters to Travellers Series Editor, Thomas Cook Publishing, PO Box 227, Coningsby Road, Peterborough PE3 8SB, UK.

Please don't forget to let us know which title your feedback refers to!